Created for Relationships

BOB DEFOOR
PAM GIBBS
SHARON GRITZ
DENNIS WILES

BAPTISTWAYPRESS®
Dallas, Texas

Created for Relationships—BaptistWay Adult Bible Study Guide®

BAPTISTWAY PRESS® Leadership Team
Executive Director, Baptist General Convention of Texas: David Hardage
Director, Church Ministry Resources: Chris Liebrum
Director, Bible Study/Discipleship Team: Phil Miller
Publisher, BaptistWay Press®: Scott Stevens

Cover and Interior Design and Production: Desktop Miracles, Inc.
Printing: Data Reproductions Corporation

First edition: June 2015
ISBN–13: 978–1–938355–36–3

How to Make the Best Use of This Issue

Whether you're the teacher or a student—

1. Start early in the week before your class meets.

2. Overview the study. Review the table of contents and read the study introduction. Try to see how each lesson relates to the overall study.

3. Use your Bible to read and consider prayerfully the Scripture passages for the lesson. (You'll see that each writer has chosen a favorite translation for the lessons in this issue. You're free to use the Bible translation you prefer and compare it with the translation chosen for that unit, of course.)

4. After reading all the Scripture passages in your Bible, then read the writer's comments. The comments are intended to be an aid to your study of the Bible.

5. Read the small articles—"sidebars"—in each lesson. They are intended to provide additional, enrichment information and inspiration and to encourage thought and application.

6. Try to answer for yourself the questions included in each lesson. They're intended to encourage further thought and application, and they can also be used in the class session itself.

If you're the teacher—

A. Do all of the things just mentioned, of course. As you begin the study with your class, be sure to find a way to help your class know the date on which each lesson will be studied. You might do this in one or more of the following ways:

   • In the first session of the study, briefly overview the study by identifying for your class the date on which each lesson will be studied. Lead your class to write the date in the table of contents on page 9 and on the first page of each lesson.

- Make and post a chart that indicates the date on which each lesson will be studied.

- If all of your class has e-mail, send them an e-mail with the dates the lessons will be studied.

- Provide a bookmark with the lesson dates. You may want to include information about your church and then use the bookmark as an outreach tool, too. A model for a bookmark can be downloaded from www.baptistwaypress.org on the **Adults— Bible Studies** page.

- Develop a sticker with the lesson dates, and place it on the table of contents or on the back cover.

- Get a copy of the *Teaching Guide*, a companion piece to this *Study Guide*. The *Teaching Guide* contains additional Bible comments plus two teaching plans. The teaching plans in the *Teaching Guide* are intended to provide practical, easy-to-use teaching suggestions that will work in your class.

B. After you've studied the Bible passage, the lesson comments, and other material, use the teaching suggestions in the *Teaching Guide* to help you develop your plan for leading your class in studying each lesson.

C. Teaching resource items for use as handouts are available free at www.baptistwaypress.org.

D. Additional Bible study comments on the lessons are available online. Call 1–866–249–1799 or e-mail baptistway@texasbaptists.org to order the *Premium Adult Online Bible Commentary*. It is available only in electronic format (PDF) from our website, www.baptistwaypress.org. The price of these comments for the entire study is $6 for individuals and $25 for a group of five. A church or class that participates in our advance order program for free shipping can receive the *Premium Adult Online Bible Commentary* free. Call 1–866–249–1799 or see www.baptistwaypress.org to purchase or for information on participating in our free shipping program for the next study.

E. Additional teaching plans are also available in electronic format (PDF) by calling 1–866–249–1799. The price of these additional teaching plans for the entire study is $5 for an individual and $20 for a group of five. A church or class that participates in our advance order program for free shipping can receive the *Premium Adult Online Teaching Plans* free. Call 1–866–249–1799 or see www.baptistwaypress.org for information on participating in our free shipping program for the next study.

F. You also may want to get the enrichment teaching help that is provided on the Internet by the *Baptist Standard* at www.baptiststandard.com. (Other class participants may find this information helpful, too.) The *Baptist Standard* is available online for an annual subscription rate of $10. Subscribe online at www.baptiststandard.com or call 214–630–4571. (A free thirty-day trial subscription is currently available.)

G. Enjoy leading your class in discovering the meaning of the Scripture passages and in applying these passages to their lives.

DO YOU USE A KINDLE?

This BaptistWay *Adult Bible Study Guide* plus *Guidance for the Seasons of Life; Living Generously for Jesus' Sake; Profiles in Character; Psalms: Songs from the Heart of Faith; Amos, Hosea, Isaiah, Micah; Jeremiah and Ezekiel; The Gospel of Matthew; The Gospel of Mark; The Gospel of Luke: Jesus' Personal Touch; The Gospel of John: Part One; The Gospel of John: Part Two; The Book of Acts: Time to Act on Acts 1:8; The Corinthian Letters: Imperatives for an Imperfect Church; Hebrews and the Letters of Peter; Letters to the Ephesians and Timothy; 14 Habits of Highly Effective Disciples; Letters to the Ephesians and Timothy; The Gospel of John; and Exodus* are now available in a Kindle edition. The easiest way to find these materials is to search for "BaptistWay" on your Kindle or go to www.amazon.com/kindle and do a search for "BaptistWay." The Kindle edition can be studied not only on a Kindle but also on a PC, Mac, iPhone, iPad, Blackberry, or Android phone using the Kindle app available free from amazon.com/kindle.

AUDIO BIBLE STUDY LESSONS

Do you want to use your walk/run/ride, etc. time to study the Bible? Or maybe you're looking for a way to study the Bible when you just can't find time to read? Or maybe you know someone who has difficulty seeing to read even our *Large Print Study Guide*?

Then try our audio Bible study lessons, available on *Living Generously for Jesus' Sake; Profiles in Character; Amos, Hosea, Isaiah, Micah; The Gospel of Matthew; The Gospel of Mark; The Gospel of Luke; The Gospel of John: Part One; The Gospel of John: Part Two; The Book of Acts; The Corinthian Letters; Galatians and 1 & 2 Thessalonians;* and *The Letters of James and John.* For more information or to order, call 1–866–249–1799 or e-mail baptistway@texasbaptists.org. The files are downloaded from our website. You'll need an audio player or phone that plays MP3 files (like an iPod®, but many MP3 players are available), or you can listen on a computer.

Writers for This Study Guide

Dennis Wiles wrote **lessons one through four.** Dennis, pastor of First Baptist Church of Arlington, Texas is husband to Cindy, father to Hannah and Josiah and Papa Dennis to Connor, Josh, and Adah. He loves all of these roles and is continually blessed through them. He lives a real life in a real family and a real church. He wouldn't have it any other way.

Sharon H. Gritz, the writer of **lessons five through seven,** is a veteran curriculum writer living in Fort Worth, Texas. She teaches adult Bible study at University Baptist Church and children's Bible study at its mission, Iglesia Bautista Luz del Mundo. Sharon earned master's and doctoral degrees from Southwestern Baptist Theological Seminary where she has taught as an adjunct professor. Her husband Paul is a retired professor of church history at Southwestern. Her daughter and son-in-law are both involved in vocational ministry.

Bob DeFoor of Harrodsburg, Kentucky wrote **lessons eight through ten.** Dr. DeFoor served more than forty years as pastor of churches in Kentucky and Georgia, serving the last twenty-eight prior to retirement as pastor of Harrodsburg Baptist Church. Both Bob and his wife Sandy are native Georgians, and both are graduates of Baylor University, Waco, Texas.

Pam Gibbs wrote **lessons eleven through thirteen.** Pam is a freelance writer and speaker who lives in Nashville, Tennessee where she serves as the youth minister at Bellevue Baptist Church. A native Texan, Pam is a graduate of Southwestern Baptist Theological Seminary and has been involved in ministry for over twenty years. She loves spending time with her husband Jim and daughter Kaitlyn.

Created for Relationships

Introducing

CREATED FOR RELATIONSHIPS

Approaching This Study of Created for Relationships

Have you ever wondered why you are here? Why has God placed you on the earth at this particular time? What is the purpose of your life? These are some weighty questions indeed. According to the Westminster Shorter Catechism, "Man's chief end is to glorify God, and to enjoy him forever."[1] The Bible speaks to these questions through the words of Jesus. He sums up the Old Testament by stating in Matthew 22:37–40:

> "Love the Lord your God with all your heart and with all your soul and with all your mind." This is the first and greatest commandment. And the second is like it: "Love your neighbor as yourself." All the Law and the Prophets hang on these two commandments.

This has come to be known as the Great Commandment. Jesus also provides marching orders for his followers through the Great Commission, found in Matthew 28:18–20:

> All authority in heaven and on earth has been given to me. Therefore go and make disciples of all nations, baptizing them in the name of the Father and of the Son and of the Holy Spirit, and teaching them to obey everything I have commanded you. And surely I am with you always, to the very end of the age.

Loving God and loving our neighbors is an outgrowth of our development as disciples of Jesus, and it motivates our efforts to make disciples of others. It seems that one of the overarching themes found in the Bible is that of *relationships*. God has created us for a relationship with him through his Son and our savior Jesus Christ, and he has also created us to be in relationship with others. In Genesis 2:18 God said, "It is not good for the man to be alone." It wasn't then and it isn't now.

This study will focus on thirteen key relationships, beginning with our relationship with God. More than ever the outside world needs to see Christians whose lives are grounded in and guided by their relationship with God. As Christ followers, we have been given the ministry of reconciliation (2 Corinthians 5:17–21). One of our primary purposes is to help people reconcile with God, whether they are family members, friends, neighbors, employers, or others in our community.

Each summer our BaptistWay Bible Study series focuses on a biblical theme. In the fall we explore material from the New Testament, in the winter we examine one of the Gospels, and in the spring we delve into an Old Testament study. For a complete list of our studies see www.baptistwaypress.org.

Studying These Lessons

Relationships can provide the most rewarding and meaningful experiences in our lives as well as some of the most trying and frustrating experiences. What is the current state of our relationships? How are we to respond to challenges in our relationships? What are some keys to building strong and lasting relationships?

The Bible provides wisdom and guidance for us in the area of relationships and this study will provide direction and suggestions for repairing and strengthening our relationships. Use the study to compare the current condition of your relationships in each area addressed with the biblical counsel. Focus on the Main Idea and Study Aim for each lesson and look for ways to practically apply the scriptural truths to your everyday life.

In the beginning God created . . .

And he created us for relationships. When God was forming his chosen people into the nation of Israel he codified instructions about relationships in the Ten Commandments: four that address our relationship with God, and six that address our relationships with others. Luke 2:52 tells us that Jesus grew in wisdom and stature, and in favor *with God and men*. Relationships are the key to a rich and meaningful life.

So how are we to relate with God, ourselves, and one another in the 21st century? Does the Bible still have anything relevant to say about our relationships with family, friends, neighbors, employers, government, church leaders, fellow Christians, and non-Christians? Absolutely it does. Our prayer is that this thirteen-week journey will shed fresh light on your relationships and will encourage you to embrace God's wisdom so that you can glorify him and enjoy your relationship with him and others.

CREATED FOR RELATIONSHIPS

Lesson 1	God	Genesis 1:26–31; Romans 5:1–11
Lesson 2	Self	1 Samuel 16:1–7; Psalm 139
Lesson 3	Spouse	Ephesians 5:21–33
Lesson 4	Children	Psalm 127:3–5; Proverbs 22:6; Deuteronomy 6:1–9
Lesson 5	Parents	Exodus 20:12; Luke 2:45–52; John 19:25–27
Lesson 6	Friends	Ecclesiastes 4:9–12; 1 Samuel 20:1–17, 27–42
Lesson 7	Enemies	Luke 6:27–36; Romans 12:17–21
Lesson 8	Neighbors/ Community	Exodus 20:13–17; Leviticus 19:16–18; Zechariah 7:8–10; Matthew 5:13–16
Lesson 9	Employer	Ephesians 6:5–9; Colossians 3:22–25; 1 Timothy 6:1–2; Titus 2:9–11
Lesson 10	Government	Romans 13:1–7; 1 Timothy 2:1–4;
Lesson 11	Church Leaders	Ephesians 4:11–16; 1 Thessalonians 5:12–13; Hebrews 13:17–18
Lesson 12	Fellow Christians	Acts 4:32–37; 1 Corinthians 12:12–27; Galatians 6:9–10; Hebrews 10:24–25
Lesson 13	Non-Christians	2 Corinthians 5:11–21; 1 Peter 3:15–16; Colossians 4:2–6

Additional Resources for Studying *Created for Relationships*[2]

Kenneth L. Barker and John R. Kohlenberger III. *The Expositor's Bible Commentary – Abridged Edition: New Testament.* Grand Rapids, Michigan: Zondervan, 1994.

Bruce Barton, Philip Comfort, Grant Osborne, Linda K. Taylor, and Dave Veerman. *Life Application New Testament Commentary.* Carol Stream, Illinois: Tyndale House Publishers, Inc., 2001.

Gary D. Chapman. *Covenant Marriage.* Nashville, TN: B&H Publishing Group, 2003.

Lon Fendall. *Citizenship: A Christian Calling.* Newberg, OR: Barclay Press, 2003.

Craig S. Keener. *IVP Bible Background Commentary: New Testament.* Downers Grove, Illinois: InterVarsity Press, 1993.

Robert S. McGee. *The Search for Significance: Seeing Your True Worth Through God's Eyes.* Nashville, TN: Thomas Nelson, 1998.

Les and Leslie Parrott. *Relationships: An Open and Honest Guide to Making Bad Relationships Better and Good Relationships Great.* Grand Rapids, MI: Zondervan, 2005.

A.T. Robertson. *Word Pictures in the New Testament: Concise Edition.* Nashville, Tennessee: Holman Bible Publishers, 2000.

Melissa Travathan and Sissy Goff. *Modern Parents, Vintage Values.* Nashville, TN: B&H Publishing Group, 2010.

Spiros Zodhiates and Warren Baker. *Hebrew-Greek Key Word Study Bible, New International Version.* Grand Rapids, Michigan: Zondervan, 1996.

NOTES

1. http://www.shortercatechism.com/resources/wsc/wsc_001.html. Accessed 7/31/14.

2. Listing a book does not imply full agreement by the writers or BAPTISTWAY PRESS® with all of its comments.

FOCAL TEXT
Genesis 1:26–31;
Romans 5:1–11

BACKGROUND
Genesis 1:26–31;
Romans 5:1–11

MAIN IDEA
God created us for
relationships and Jesus
has reconciled our
relationship with God.

QUESTION TO EXPLORE
What does it mean to be
created in God's image, and
how has Jesus reconciled our
relationship with God?

STUDY AIM
To comprehend what it
means to be created in God's
image and to understand
how Jesus provides
reconciliation with God

QUICK READ
God has revealed himself as
a personal God. He created
human beings in his image
with a unique capacity to
live in relationship with
each other and with him.

LESSON ONE
God

Introduction

Seated on a mat outside a mud-brick hut in West Africa, I was engaged in a serious theological discussion with the local imam (Muslim cleric) in the village. Through a translator, we compared the teachings of the Bible with those of the Koran. Because my group had been to this village numerous times, the two of us shared a great deal of trust and therefore could talk freely.

At one point in the discussion, the imam asked about the purpose of humanity. "Why did God place us here?" He acknowledged me as a "holy man" for Americans, even though he didn't quite understand my role as a pastor. In spite of his limited exposure to Christianity, he still pondered the deeper questions of life. Why did he pose such an important, life-altering question? Because he is human.

The imam's question is one of purpose. Why *did* God create each of us? What was God's original intent? What was his desire for humanity? How did he express those desires in the design of his creation? Furthermore, what happened to God's plan? Why is there so much brokenness in the human story? What went wrong? And further still, what did God do about this brokenness? How has God responded to the presence of sin and evil?

These profound questions are worth exploring. We can't definitively answer all of them in one Bible study, but we can lay a strong foundation for deeper understanding. The only way we can understand our purpose is in light of God's character. The Bible paints a portrait of God as a personal being. He is not an abstract being existent in another far-off dimension. He is not aloof or indifferent. Instead, the Bible reveals God as active and engaged in his creation. He speaks, acts, feels, loves, listens, cares, and knows.[1]

GENESIS 1:26–31

[26] Then God said, "Let us make man in our image, in our likeness, and let them rule over the fish of the sea and the birds of the air, over the livestock, over all the earth, and over all the creatures that move along the ground."

[27] So God created man in his own image,

> in the image of God he created him;
> male and female he created them.

²⁸ God blessed them and said to them, "Be fruitful and increase in number; fill the earth and subdue it. Rule over the fish of the sea and the birds of the air and over every living creature that moves on the ground."

²⁹ Then God said, "I give you every seed-bearing plant on the face of the whole earth and every tree that has fruit with seed in it. They will be yours for food. ³⁰ And to all the beasts of the earth and all the birds of the air and all the creatures that move on the ground—everything that has the breath of life in it—I give every green plant for food." And it was so.

³¹ God saw all that he had made, and it was very good. And there was evening, and there was morning—the sixth day.

ROMANS 5:1–11

¹ Therefore, since we have been justified through faith, we have peace with God through our Lord Jesus Christ, ² through whom we have gained access by faith into this grace in which we now stand. And we rejoice in the hope of the glory of God. ³ Not only so, but we also rejoice in our sufferings, because we know that suffering produces perseverance; ⁴ perseverance, character; and character, hope. ⁵ And hope does not disappoint us, because God has poured out his love into our hearts by the Holy Spirit, whom he has given us.

⁶ You see, at just the right time, when we were still powerless, Christ died for the ungodly. ⁷ Very rarely will anyone die for a righteous man, though for a good man someone might possibly dare to die. ⁸ But God demonstrates his own love for us in this: While we were still sinners, Christ died for us.

⁹ Since we have now been justified by his blood, how much more shall we be saved from God's wrath through him! ¹⁰ For if, when we were God's enemies, we were reconciled to him through the death of his Son, how much more, having been reconciled, shall we be saved through his life! ¹¹ Not only is this so, but we also rejoice in God through our Lord Jesus Christ, through whom we have now received reconciliation.

God is a Complex Being (Genesis 1:26–31)

Genesis 1:26–31 contains material essential to understanding the entire Bible. The Creator of the universe decided to populate planet earth with human beings. These beings have been specifically designed with unique capabilities and responsibilities. They obviously matter to God since he spoke directly only to them. He did not address the rest of creation. However, he spoke to human beings.

Genesis 1:26 utilizes the plural in reference to God. Notice the phrase "Let us make man in our image, in our likeness." The Old Testament often refers to God in the plural (we, our, us), rather than the singular (I, mine, me). For example, the Bible opens with a declarative statement, "In the beginning God created the heavens and the earth." The Hebrew word for "God" in this verse is *Elohim*, which is a plural noun. However, the word for "create" is in the singular. In addition, this passage also utilizes the pronouns "us" and "our" with reference to God. Some scholars have proposed that the plural usage refers to the heavenly host surrounding and accompanying God at creation. However, this would imply that God had "assistance" in the creative process. This idea is not in agreement with the rest of the Bible (See Isaiah 40:25–26; Hebrews 1:10–12). The Bible clearly presents God as the sole Creator of the universe.

Other scholars believe that the writer used plural nouns and pronouns to express God's "plural majesty." To these scholars, the plural allowed

THE IMAGO DEI

In the New Testament, the Greek word for "image" is *character*. This word referred to a stamp or an impression on a seal or coin. It was a representation of the original design. Jesus Christ is the perfect representation of God the Father (Heb. 1:1–4). Because Jesus was sinless, he most accurately bore God's image and reflected God's glory in our world. Our sin hinders us from fully bearing the image of God. However, God is at work in us to restore his image. His power can transform our brokenness and sinfulness so we can reflect his glory. He desires to conform us to the likeness of his Son (Rom. 8:29). We will never be perfect. We will never be completely free from sin this side of heaven. But, we can become more like Jesus.

the writer of Genesis to express the inexpressible, since there is no way to describe God adequately and fully within the limits of language. Thus, one way to set God apart is to refer to him in the plural. However, using the plural to show God's majesty falls short. The name *Elohim* is a common word for God in the Old Testament. It occurs about 4,000 times in the Old Testament. Further, another word for God is *Adonai*, translated as "Lord." It is also a plural noun and is found numerous times in the Old Testament (Gen. 18:30; Exodus 34:23; Deuteronomy 10:17; Psalm 45:11; 114:7; Malachi 1:6).

The plural nouns and pronouns used in the Old Testament point to a greater reality expressed in the New Testament and further developed in early Christian theology. God exists in eternity, in community *and* plurality. And yet, he is one God. The New Testament clearly references the Father, Son, and Spirit as all being divine (Matthew 28:16–20; John 8:58; 1 Corinthians 12:4–6; Ephesians 4:4–6). God is a complex Being. He is one God who exists in plurality. He is not like us. He is God. Sovereign. Majestic. Glorious. Complex.

Humanity: God's Crowning Achievement (Genesis 1:26–31)

Genesis 1:26–31 also reveals abiding truths about human beings. God created human beings in his image (*Imago Dei* in Latin) and according to his likeness. "Image" and "likeness" are two closely related terms. Though some scholars break down and analyze these two words to draw up distinctions between them, they communicate truths that reinforce one another. Being created in God's image and likeness means humans are moral creatures capable of knowing right and wrong. They have the unique capacity to represent God and his causes in creation. This truth speaks to the unique nature of human beings. They are the only image-bearers of God in the vastness of creation.

God's image and likeness also enable human beings to relate to God. God expressed his desire for this relationship in Genesis 1:27–30. He spoke to human beings. He expressed his intent for them to multiply and rule over the earth. Humans hold the capacity to know God and follow his commands. Human beings have the unique opportunity to respond directly to his desires. In other words, God created human beings and invited them to live in relationship with him.

Since God exists in eternity in relationship as a complex being of Father, Son, and Holy Spirit, he designed human beings as relational creatures as well. He created humanity as male and female. The complementary nature of the genders is evident from the very beginning (Gen. 2:18–25). Both genders express more fully God's image and likeness than one gender alone. He invited human beings to join him in caring for and ruling over his creation. Humans care for it since it belongs to him—and so do we. Once God brought human beings into existence, blessed them and charged them, he pronounced his assessment of his creative activity. It was all very good (1:31).

The Answer to Our Brokenness (Romans 5:1–11)

Genesis 2 ends in perfection. Human beings (Adam and Eve) existed in perfect harmony with God, creation, and each other. However, the third chapter of the Bible introduces the tragic story of humanity's rebellion and sin, for which God judged his unique creatures. They would still bear his image in the world (Gen. 9:6), but their ability to do so as God desired had been marred.

They were cast out of the Garden of Eden to live in a newly broken world. However, God had already set into place a plan to restore his crowning creation back to himself. His answer to the judgment, separation, guilt, and pain of humanity's rebellion was redemption. God decided to redeem humanity from final judgment in hell and to offer humans the opportunity to serve his purposes on earth. However, redemption required sin's debt to be paid—at the highest price.

In Romans 5:1–11, Paul explained God's plan of redemption and rescue. Death and separation from God-deserving punishment characterized the human predicament (Romans 3:23; Ephesians 2:1–3). Not surprisingly, God responded personally. He sent his Son, the perfect Image-Bearer (Heb. 1:1–4), to bring peace between human beings and God.

Humanity stands condemned before God. However, because of the person and work of Jesus Christ, we can be justified. We can be declared innocent before God because Jesus, the Son of God, has atoned for humanity's sin. God no longer declares us guilty if we call on Christ as Savior. He justifies those who turn to him in repentance and faith.

TO DO THIS WEEK:

1. People around you live with a broken relationship with God. Many of them have never heard about God at all. You can demonstrate to them how a redeemed person lives. God can use you at home, at work, and in your everyday life to represent him.

2. Ask God to reveal to you his perspective of your family, workplace, neighborhood, church, and circle of friends. Ask him to show you how to bear his image in each of these spheres of influence.

Justification is a concept from the legal realm of the first century. God the Judge has declared us innocent, not because of what we have accomplished, but because of Christ's work on the cross.

Romans 5:1–11 explains the beautiful effects of this justification. The saving work of Christ has brought peace (5:1). Christians can now rejoice in hope (5:2). We are not separated from God any longer. We have been granted access to him (5:2). We do not sit as accused, but now stand in the grace of God. This standing before God is all God's doing. Human beings could do nothing about their sin and its accompanying judgment. He personally intervened in our situation and provided the only solution to our need.

Our relationship with God can be restored through Christ. However, we still live in a broken world. He has not exempted us from the tragedies and suffering that afflict all human beings (5:3–5). Even though we have peace with God, we must still navigate the choppy waters of a sinful, fallen world. Suffering will still accompany us on the journey. However, God can use that suffering as a way for us to experience and express his love and grace. We can bear up in our circumstances and benefit from them. God can produce qualities like perseverance through our hardships. Believers can live as examples of his grace and love in the face of life's challenges.

Paul reminded his readers that this salvation is real and historically verifiable. Jesus Christ was sent by God to accomplish the salvation of humanity (5:6–8). God responded to the sinfulness of humanity (Gen. 3) by providing a way of true salvation. At just the precise time (Rom. 5:6), God sent his Son into the world to accomplish the miracle of salvation (Galatians 4:4). Salvation flows from the heart of the Creator (Rom. 5:8). Because of his personal love for his creatures, God has offered them the opportunity to be reconciled to him and saved from the penalty and power of sin (5:9–11).

Implications and Actions

God created human beings to live in relationship with him. He designed us as relational creatures. However, sin separated humanity from God and damaged this relationship. God responded to this brokenness through a personal and sacrificial expression of love. At just the right time, God sent his Son to redeem humanity from its condition and to reconcile humans back to him. As a result, we can bear his image in a broken world as he uses us as instruments of restoration and healing. God wants to use believers as his image-bearers to communicate the message of reconciliation and hope to our world. We have the unique opportunity to fulfill his original desires for us.

QUESTIONS

1. How would you explain to someone what it means to be made in the image of God?

2. How does the Bible present God as a relational God?

3. As you think about the meaning of the focal passages, what has God shown you about his image and likeness in your life?

4. Reflect upon God's gift of salvation. How is God's grace at work in your life in your personal relationship with him?

5. How can Christians bear God's image as they interact with a
   broken world?

NOTES ———————————————————————————————

1. Unless otherwise indicated, all Scripture quotations in lessons 1–4 and 8–13 are from the
   New International Version (1984 edition).

LESSON TWO
Self

FOCAL TEXT
1 Samuel 16:1–7; Psalm 139

BACKGROUND
1 Samuel 16:1–7; Psalm 139

MAIN IDEA
Our identity and worth are found in what God says about us.

QUESTION TO EXPLORE
What is the source of my identity and worth?

STUDY AIM
To define my identity and worth based on what God says about me

QUICK READ
Human beings often allow outward appearances to dictate their worth. God's unique love for us ought to establish our worth.

Introduction

I've always been interested in the royal family of England. My first visit to London was highlighted by seeing Her Majesty, the Queen at a ceremony at St. Paul's Cathedral. A few years later, I joined others around the world in grieving when Princess Diana died. I watched the live broadcast of her funeral on television. I'll never forget it. I thought about the day that I saw the Queen and reflected upon the life of the royals.

A few days later, I also grieved with others when Mother Teresa died. I watched the live broadcast of her funeral as well. It was moving. However, during the airing one commentator said, "I was in attendance at Princess Diana's funeral, and I am here at Mother Teresa's as well. I must say that the funeral of the Princess was much more impressive than that of Mother Teresa."

The statement left me dumbfounded. I know what the commentator meant. Mother Teresa's procession traveled through the muddy streets of an Indian city with much less pomp and circumstance than Princess Diana's glorious display of royalty and honor. The comment demonstrated our culture's obsession with outward appearance, dignitaries, and perceived power. What about you? Are you moved by outward appearances? Does someone's status in the community or culture impress you?

1 SAMUEL 16:1–7

The LORD said to Samuel, "How long will you mourn for Saul, since I have rejected him as king over Israel? Fill your horn with oil and be on your way; I am sending you to Jesse of Bethlehem. I have chosen one of his sons to be king."

[2] But Samuel said, "How can I go? Saul will hear about it and kill me."

The LORD said, "Take a heifer with you and say, 'I have come to sacrifice to the LORD.' [3] Invite Jesse to the sacrifice, and I will show you what to do. You are to anoint for me the one I indicate."

[4] Samuel did what the LORD said. When he arrived at Bethlehem, the elders of the town trembled when they met him. They asked, "Do you come in peace?"

[5] Samuel replied, "Yes, in peace; I have come to sacrifice to the

LORD. Consecrate yourselves and come to the sacrifice with me." Then he consecrated Jesse and his sons and invited them to the sacrifice.

⁶ When they arrived, Samuel saw Eliab and thought, "Surely the LORD's anointed stands here before the LORD."

⁷ But the LORD said to Samuel, "Do not consider his appearance or his height, for I have rejected him. The LORD does not look at the things man looks at. Man looks at the outward appearance, but the LORD looks at the heart."

PSALM 139

¹ O LORD, you have searched me
    and you know me.
² You know when I sit and when I rise;
    you perceive my thoughts from afar.
³ You discern my going out and my lying down;
    you are familiar with all my ways.
⁴ Before a word is on my tongue
    you know it completely, O LORD.
⁵ You hem me in—behind and before;
    you have laid your hand upon me.
⁶ Such knowledge is too wonderful for me,
    too lofty for me to attain.
⁷ Where can I go from your Spirit?
    Where can I flee from your presence?
⁸ If I go up to the heavens, you are there;
    if I make my bed in the depths, you are there.
⁹ If I rise on the wings of the dawn,
    if I settle on the far side of the sea,
¹⁰ even there your hand will guide me,
    your right hand will hold me fast.
¹¹ If I say, "Surely the darkness will hide me
    and the light become night around me,"
¹² even the darkness will not be dark to you;
    the night will shine like the day,
    for darkness is as light to you.

13 For you created my inmost being;
   you knit me together in my mother's womb.
14 I praise you because I am fearfully and wonderfully made;
   your works are wonderful,
   I know that full well.
15 My frame was not hidden from you
   when I was made in the secret place.
   When I was woven together in the depths of the earth,
16 your eyes saw my unformed body.
   All the days ordained for me were written in your book
   before one of them came to be.
17 How precious to me are your thoughts, O God!
   How vast is the sum of them!
18 Were I to count them,
   they would outnumber the grains of sand.
   When I awake, I am still with you.
19 If only you would slay the wicked, O God!
   Away from me, you bloodthirsty men!
20 They speak of you with evil intent;
   your adversaries misuse your name.
21 Do I not hate those who hate you, O LORD,
   and abhor those who rise up against you?
22 I have nothing but hatred for them;
   I count them my enemies.
23 Search me, O God, and know my heart;
   test me and know my anxious thoughts.
24 See if there is any offensive way in me,
   and lead me in the way everlasting.

Background—A King for Israel

By his power, God rescued Israel from years of slavery in Egypt. He used Moses as the human instrument for this rescue mission. This mighty man of God led Israel for forty years in the wilderness subsequent to the miraculous deliverance from Egypt. After Moses died, Joshua led Israel into the land promised to Abraham. The land of Canaan became home to this fledgling nation.

The nation was divided geographically by tribe. God made the assignments. For many years, Israel existed as a tribal confederation ruled by judges. These men and women demonstrated military skill and leadership ability. They led the people of God as they settled into life in this Promised Land.

However, being led by God became unpopular. Envying the pagan nations around it, Israel longed for a king. They wanted an earthly ruler to whom they could pay homage. In those days, God spoke through a prophet and priest named Samuel. He was the spiritual conscience of the nation. God led him to anoint a man named Saul as the first king of Israel. Saul was an imposing physical figure who stood a head taller than everyone else. However, Saul was prone to bouts of depression and fits of rage. He was not reliable. Further, he disobeyed God. In the verses prior to the focal passage for this study, God judged Saul and rejected him as king of Israel. His family would not be the royal family for Israel.

Samuel had anointed Saul as king. He mourned over Saul's failures (1 Samuel 15:35). God confronted Samuel and called him to anoint a new king for Israel. That is where we pick up the story in our focal passage. A new royal family was about to be brought onto center stage.

Outward Appearances vs. Inward Realities (1 Samuel 16:1–7)

Samuel knew how unpredictable and volatile Saul could be. Consequently, when God came to Samuel and directed him to crown a new king of Israel, he resisted. In fact, he admitted to God that he was afraid Saul would kill him if Saul knew he was going to anoint a new king.

Nevertheless, God sent Samuel to Jesse's family in Bethlehem. Jesse was of the tribe of Judah and a descendant of Ruth and Boaz (Ruth 4:22). The Jews believed the Messiah would come from this tribe. Certainly Samuel knew this. God met Samuel's apprehension with a plan. He told Samuel to take a sacrifice with him. No one would suspect anything suspicious if a priest showed up with a sacrifice.

Samuel obeyed God. The leaders in Bethlehem knew Samuel and the power he had exhibited in other settings (1 Sam. 15:32–33). They were afraid of him. In verse 5, Samuel had to set their minds at ease. While he prepared the sacrifice, he met Jesse and one of Jesse's sons. He knew God

WHO WAS JOHN BROADUS?

John Broadus (1827–1895) is recognized as one of the greatest preachers in Southern Baptist history. He was on the founding faculty of The Southern Baptist Theological Seminary, served as president of the seminary (1889–1895), and preached to Robert E. Lee's army. He baptized legendary missionary Lottie Moon, was sought out by John D. Rockefeller to pastor his church in New York, and was called the "greatest living preacher" by Charles Spurgeon. He was truly one of the finest leaders in Baptist history.

On one occasion, he was preaching in a rural church in South Carolina. Already a popular preacher, seminary professor, and recognized Baptist leader, he was hoping to raise funds from this church to support the seminary. After he had begun preaching that Sunday, a farmer slipped in the back of the church and took his seat. He had not heard the pastor's glowing introduction of Broadus. After the sermon, the farmer shook Broadus' hand and said, "Great sermon. If you get some more education, you may amount to something."

Broadus took that statement as a great compliment. He received a genuine word of blessing from a farmer who had no idea who Broadus was. Broadus did not try to impress people with an outward demonstration of his vast education and superior preaching skills. He recognized that his value stemmed from God's unconditional love and saving power, not his impressive resume.

had chosen one of his sons to be the new king (1 Sam. 16:1). After meeting Eliab, Samuel assumed God would choose Jesse's eldest. Samuel was impressed by what he saw (16:6). Remember, Samuel had anointed Saul, who was quite a physical specimen (1 Sam. 9:1–2). Evidently, Samuel was looking for a replacement with similar physical attributes.

God answered Samuel with one of the most insightful statements in the Old Testament. He explained to Samuel that he does not judge according to outward appearance, but instead he looks upon a person's heart (1 Sam. 16:7).

In Samuel's day—and our day—too much attention is paid to outward appearances. People are easily impressed, but God is not. We can learn a valuable lesson here. Believers should not be so easily impressed by fame, fortune, or earthly power and influence. These characteristics are all fleeting, transient, and prone to change and corruption. Our identity as image-bearers of God is not determined by these outward manifestations of worth. They are not deep enough. Our worth is not tied to accomplishments or human approval. Our identity rests in God's creating us as his children. Our worth stems from what God thinks about us, not what we (or others) think about us. He looks at the heart. He is not impressed with the car we drive or the house we own. He wants our commitment and loyalty to him and his purposes. That is what matters.

Background—A King and a Poet

Samuel anointed Jesse's youngest son, David, as the next king of Israel. His leadership became world renowned. The prophets referred to the Messiah as the Son of David (Matthew 21:1–11). He was the prototype against whom all future kings would be compared. He received the ultimate compliment as a man "after God's own heart" (Acts 13:22).

David was a poet and musician, a talented instrumentalist and writer. The Book of Psalms has served as an expression of worship for God's people for centuries. It contains hymns, poems, prophecies, and prayers. It contains 150 individual poems, and traditional scholars attribute David as the author of over seventy of them.

A Personal God (Psalm 139:1–6)

Most students of the Bible attribute Psalm 139 to David. It beautifully describes and characterizes God as the Creator of the universe, including every human being. It is a hymn that contains both thanksgiving and lament.

The first four verses of Psalm 139 declare God to be a personal God. He knows every intimate and intricate detail of every person's life. He knows when we sit down and stand up (139:2a). He knows our thoughts while they are still incubating (139:2b). He knows when we travel and when we are still (139:3). In fact, he knows what we will say before the words leave our lips (139:4). Nothing in our lives escapes his watchful eye and protective care (139:5). These verses do not describe a God who

LIVE OUT THE TRUTH THIS WEEK:

1. Each day, thank God for one unique quality you possess (not based on outward appearances).

2. As you encounter people who are not like you (from the rich man to the pauper), ask yourself: Have I judged this person on outward appearance?

3. Send a note to a friend who needs to remember that God knows every detail of their life, so they can trust him amidst a difficult experience.

4. Memorize any verses from our focal passages that spoke to you this week. You might memorize 1 Samuel 16:7 or Psalm 139:7–10.

stands in the background, aloof and unconcerned with our daily lives. Rather, he knows us better than we know ourselves. Notice how many times either the word "know" or its derivative "knowledge" is used in the opening verses. Our God *knows* us.

A Sovereign God (Psalm 139:7–12)

After acknowledging the intimacy of God's knowledge about humanity, David quickly pointed out God's sovereignty over the entire universe. In verses 7–12, he outlined the comprehensive nature of God's knowledge and activity. With sweeping language, David expressed his absolute inability to escape the presence of God at any time (139:7–9). God is everywhere, all the time. Even when we feel the darkness threatening to overwhelm us, God dispels the darkness.

To God, there is no difference between night and day. Neither can one limit his ability to see our lives as they unfold. In those midnight hours, God leads us. He can see in the dark even when it blinds us. Nothing in our lives is beyond God's guardian hand (139:10–12). This powerful truth can provide comfort and peace for God's children. He is always with us. His protective care cannot be contained.

This declaration of the vast and all-encompassing sovereignty of God, paired with God's intimate knowledge of our lives point to God's loving concern for us. We matter to God. He cares deeply about us. God's determination to know us deeply and care for us extensively demonstrates his love and concern for each individual. Our search for worth thirsts for this truth and assurance. Influenced by celebrity culture and altars built to fortune and accomplishment, our world needs to know the truth about identity and worth. We are valuable to God. Regardless of our stock portfolio, trophy case, marital status, or sinful past, God loves and cares for us. Remember, he looks at the heart (1 Sam. 16:7).

Created for a Purpose (Psalm 139:13–18)

In a stunning revelation, David extended God's sovereignty to the mother's womb. No human being is an accident. In verse 13, David declared God as the Architect of our souls and the Designer of our bodies. He created us as both physical and spiritual creatures. In doing so, he demonstrated his sovereignty over all life. He is the Life-giver. His handiwork is on display in the heavens (Ps. 19) as well as in the womb.

Once again, his presence in our lives (even before our birth) points to the worth of each human being. In verse 14, the psalmist used two words to describe how God designed us: fearfully and wonderfully. The word "fearfully" is derived from the word "fear" that is often found in the Old Testament. We read in Proverbs that the "fear of the LORD is the beginning of knowledge" (Proverbs 1:7). In these instances, "fear" means "respect, reverence, or awe."

In Psalm 139:14, David declared that God has shown great reverence and respect for life, for every life. He is so interested in each human being that he is reverently involved in every aspect of their lives, even their formation and development prenatally. In verse 14, the word translated "wonderfully" means "unique" or "marvelous." Again, these words point to the worth of each human being. God designed each person uniquely and with great attention to every detail.

In the closing verses, the psalmist declared God's purposeful plan for every person. God has "ordained" our days (139:16) and created us to fulfill his purposes. He desires for us to live in relationship with him and to serve him. This recognition of God's masterful creativity, his intimate involvement in all aspects of life, and his sovereignty left David on his knees, declaring God's ways far beyond our understanding (139:17–18).

Implications and Actions

Do you realize just how much God values, cherishes, prizes, and cares about you? Do you think you must accomplish something great for him so he will love you? If you have bought into this lie, this psalm can speak directly to you. God paid attention to you while you were still in your mother's womb, even before your cells had begun dividing to create you. Even then, his love was already present in your life.

Does God want us to live for him? Yes. Does our performance earn his love and increase our value in his eyes? Absolutely not. Too often, we as Christians confuse the terms of our relationship and service to God. We love and live for him because we have experienced his undeserved, unrelenting love for us—not in order to earn and receive it. His love was present long before we could give him anything in return. We are valuable to God because he made us, not because we are stellar examples of godliness. Our identity is based on his love for us, not our accomplishments.

QUESTIONS

1. What does this psalm teach you about your worth?

2. How does this psalm differ from the world's perception of worth?

3. Why is it important to know that God looks at the heart and not outward appearances?

4. How have you made judgments based on outward appearances? How have you been judged based on your outward characteristics?

5. How would you describe the worth of any human being based on what you have learned?

FOCAL TEXT
Ephesians 5:21–33

BACKGROUND
Ephesians 5:1–33

MAIN IDEA
Spouses who treat each other
with mutual love and respect
model the relationship of
Christ to his church.

QUESTION TO EXPLORE
How should marriage model
the relationship between
Christ and his church?

STUDY AIM
To choose to model my
marriage on the relationship
between Christ and his church.

QUICK READ
Marriage is a sacred institution
that reflects the covenantal
relationship between
Christ and his church.

LESSON THREE
Spouse

Introduction

Having served as a pastor since 1983, I have officiated at many weddings. Just this past summer, I performed eleven weddings! I love them. The occasion allows me to be invested personally in the lives of individuals and families at a memorable time in their lives.

One of my favorite weddings took place between two young people from Nigeria. The bride belonged to one of the royal families of that nation. Her grandfather is the king over their region of the country. Her father is a prince and she is a princess. The wedding was quite an event. Our church was filled with Nigerians.

When the father escorted his daughter down the aisle, the congregation stood and then bowed when the prince walked by them. It was an incredibly reverent act. When I asked, "Who gives this woman to be married to this man?" the father paused and faced the congregation. He introduced himself with his royal title. The congregation applauded. He faced the groom and asked him, "Do you understand the sacredness of your role? Are you prepared to embrace your sacred duty and enter the royal family?"

"Yes," the groom replied.

"Are you ready to pledge your life as a husband to my daughter?"

"I am," the groom replied. The African prince turned to me and said, "I grant my consent." He placed his daughter's hand in the hand of the groom and took a seat.

As I watched this scene unfold, I was reminded again of the sacred nature of marriage. This African father was serious in his manner and somber in his tone. Giving away his daughter was no laughing matter. The sacredness of that moment has stayed with me ever since.

EPHESIANS 5:21–33

21 Submit to one another out of reverence for Christ.

22 Wives, submit to your husbands as to the Lord. 23 For the husband is the head of the wife as Christ is the head of the church, his body, of which he is the Savior. 24 Now as the church submits to Christ, so also wives should submit to their husbands in everything.

[25] Husbands, love your wives, just as Christ loved the church and gave himself up for her [26] to make her holy, cleansing her by the washing with water through the word, [27] and to present her to himself as a radiant church, without stain or wrinkle or any other blemish, but holy and blameless. [28] In this same way, husbands ought to love their wives as their own bodies. He who loves his wife loves himself. [29] After all, no one ever hated his own body, but he feeds and cares for it, just as Christ does the church— [30] for we are members of his body. [31] "For this reason a man will leave his father and mother and be united to his wife, and the two will become one flesh." [32] This is a profound mystery—but I am talking about Christ and the church. [33] However, each one of you also must love his wife as he loves himself, and the wife must respect her husband.

Background: Preparing for Marriage

My wife and I have prepared for three weddings: our own, our daughter's, and our son's. Each wedding held its own uniqueness. Through those weddings, I learned that preparation is a necessity for the wedding to be successful. Preparation is even more crucial to the success of the marriage. The wedding is over in one weekend. The marriage lasts for life.

The Holy Spirit led Paul to discuss marital relationships in his letter to the church at Ephesus. Our focal passage, Ephesians 5:21–33, contains his instructions concerning this foundational relationship. However, his teachings about marriage are placed contextually in a broader discussion. If we want to understand Paul's line of thought, we must prepare ourselves a bit. We must set the context of the letter. In Ephesians 5:15, Paul admonished his readers to "be very careful, then, how you live." He then outlined three applications of this admonition: don't be unwise, don't be foolish, and don't get drunk with wine. On the positive side, he offered three contrasts: be wise, understand God's will, and be filled with the Spirit (Eph. 5:15–18).

Beginning in verse 18, the Greek text of Ephesians forms one long sentence that ends in verse 21. Along with the two commands (don't

POLYGAMY IN THE BIBLE

Does the Bible promote polygamy? Aren't there examples of polygamy in the Bible?

Because I am a pastor, people often ask me about polygamy
any time I preach on the biblical perspective of marriage. Actually,
polygamy does exist in the Bible. The earliest example is in Genesis
4:19, when Lamech took two wives—Adah and Zillah. This is the first
mention of this practice in human history.

As the story of the Bible unfolds, it records numerous examples
of polygamy. In fact, some prominent men in Scripture practiced it,
including Jacob, David, and Solomon. However, a careful reading
of the biblical text reveals that God never commanded polygamy
or blessed it. God never instructed anyone to take for himself more
than one wife. He never condoned or encouraged the practice of
polygamy.

Further, the Bible is honest in its accounting of the events it
records. Multiple wives often resulted in brokenness and difficult
family relationships. For example, Joseph's brothers hated him
because he was his father's favorite son. He was the son of Rachel,
whom Jacob loved, while the other sons were born to Leah, his other
wife. The dysfunction in this family is at least somewhat connected
to Jacob's decision to take on multiple wives and concubines.

get drunk with wine, and be filled with the Spirit), the text contains
five phrases that illustrate how a Spirit-filled person lives: speaking to
each other with psalms, hymns, and spiritual songs; singing; making
music; giving thanks; and submitting to each other in the fear of Christ.
The English translation of this one sentence has been broken down into
manageable units of thought. Five sentences offer six commands. The
command to be filled with the Spirit is demonstrated by the behaviors
listed in the passage.

After the Honeymoon (Ephesians 5:21–25)

Relevant to our discussion is the command to be filled with the Spirit.
In verse 21, one of the characteristics of a Spirit-filled believer is a

willingness to be submissive. We are to submit to each other out of reverence for Christ. We are to "lean toward" each other, recognizing and sensing the needs of each other.

Paul contextualized the discussion of marriage within the larger concept of submission. God calls Christians to be Spirit-filled and mutually submissive to one another, recognizing the value of others' perspectives and opinions. Paul challenged the wives to "lean toward" their own husbands. The word "submit" in verse 22 is actually not present in the Greek text. The text could read, "Submit to one another out of reverence for Christ. Wives to your own husbands as unto the Lord."

This submission is a voluntary action on a wife's behalf. She chooses to be submissive. Paul used the imagery of the relationship between the church and Christ to illustrate his point (Eph. 5:23–24). Paul challenged husbands to be spiritual leaders in the home. Again, Christ provides the example. Husbands should demonstrate a loving, servant-oriented spirit as leaders—just as Christ did.

In fact, Ephesians 5:25 contains a radical admonition from Paul. In the ancient world, husbands did not always love their wives. Wives were often viewed as child-bearers and homemakers. The affections of a husband and his sexual activities were often extra-marital. Many of the pagan temples included sexual promiscuity as a part of their ritualistic worship. Pagan men participated freely and without reprisal. Against that backdrop, Paul challenged Christian husbands to abide by a higher standard and a higher calling—to love unconditionally.

The Greek language of Paul's day was more robust than the English language. New Testament Greek contained several words for the concept of love. The word *eros* was the most common word for love. It refers to a sensual or sexual love. It is found throughout Greek literature but never occurs in the Greek New Testament. Another word for love was *philia*, translated as "affection" or "love." This love refers to familial love or affection. Paul did not use either of these two words translated as "love." Rather, he used a third word for love—*agape*. It means "unconditional love." This is the word used throughout the New Testament to signify God's love. Paul exhorted Christian husbands to demonstrate unconditional love toward their wives, following the example of Christ, who loved unconditionally and sacrificed himself willingly for the sake of others.

In verse 25, Paul proclaimed that Christ loves the church and made the ultimate sacrifice for her. Paul portrayed Christ as a groom or husband.

Just as he has served the church and loved it sacrificially, Christian husbands are to love their wives and serve them sacrificially. This kind of love is transformative, selfless, and humbling.

The marriage relationship is a partnership between a husband and a wife. It is not an employer-employee relationship. Husbands are not bosses, but rather leaders. Wives also assume leadership roles in marriage. Couples bring different strengths to the relationship. Because they mutually submit to each other (Eph. 5:21), they learn to use each other's strengths in ways that benefit the marriage. Exercising leadership utilizes strengths and serves the overall good. True leadership in the home is not about winning battles and exerting individual wills. Such action contradicts the example of Christ.

Christ and the Church (Ephesians 5:26–33)

Paul used the imagery of Christ and the church to demonstrate the covenantal nature of marriage. It is a deeply binding bond rooted in love and mutual respect. It is also a spiritual union. In verses 26–27, Paul used part of an ancient hymn to deepen his conversation about marriage. The spiritual union between a husband and wife is comparable to Christ's relationship with the church. He has cleansed the church and is preparing the church for a future celebration in eternity. This brief hymn quotation was probably familiar to the readers in Paul's day.

Husbands and wives experience the beauty of intimacy that is only attainable in marriage. Their lives are joined together in a deep bond that defies definition or full description (Eph. 5:28–29). A mystery surrounds this union. The same is true with Christ and the church. Paul then called his readers to remember the first marriage (Eph. 5:31). Adam and Eve first experienced this one-flesh relationship as husband and wife. Two lives merge together in a marriage. The spiritual, emotional, and physical intimacy between a married couple is unparalleled in any other human relationship. The depth of connection transcends the physical expression of sexuality and encompasses every facet of one's life. It is a beautiful experience of harmony that is illustrative of the mysterious connection Christ has with the church.

The relationship between Christ and the church is similar to Old Testament images of God's relationship to Israel. On several occasions,

CHURCHES CAN ASSIST MARRIED COUPLES IN NUMEROUS WAYS:

1. Host and promote seminars and retreats for married couples.
2. Provide opportunities for married couples to serve together in ministry.
3. Provide resources that deal with specific challenges married couples face.
4. Preach and teach regularly on marriage and marriage enrichment.
5. Train older, more experienced couples to serve as mentors for younger couples.
6. Enlist couples to lead the church family in worship.

God referred to himself as a groom and Israel as his bride (Isaiah 54:5, 61:10, 62:5). This human depiction enabled Israel to better comprehend the love God had for her as a nation. The focal passage reaffirms this understanding of God's relationship with his people, while also challenging married couples to mirror this covenant type of love.

Implications and Actions

Marriage is a hotly debated topic in our culture. Across our nation, various groups want to amend, change, alter, and redefine marriage. Many people no longer view marriage as a sacred institution, but rather a cultural rite of passage and a legal status. It has become a disposable relationship of convenience. Consequently, divorce continues to be a viable and valid alternative for struggling couples, and it tears apart many families.

As Christians, we must follow scriptural guidance and directives in these challenging times. We cannot allow the culture to define, redefine, or defame marriage. The Bible is clear: marriage is between one man and one woman for a lifetime. This one-flesh relationship is characterized by service and sacrifice. As believers, we must take more seriously our commitment to marriage. As a church, we must prepare couples better for the married life ahead of them. We must help families deal with the real demands that often weaken marriages. Leading people to understand the spiritual, physical, and emotional union in marriage that is modeled on the relationship between Christ and the church is a good place to start.

QUESTIONS

1. How would you describe the current state of marriage in our culture?

2. How would you explain the connection between marriage and the relationship between Christ and the church?

3. What are some ways Christians can better model marriage for our culture?

4. How can husbands and wives demonstrate healthy partnerships in their marriages?

5. What outside forces threaten the strength and solidarity of your marriage?

6. What steps do you need to take in order to strengthen your marriage?

FOCAL TEXT
Psalm 127:3–5; Proverbs
22:6; Deuteronomy 6:1–9

BACKGROUND
Psalm 127:1–5; Proverbs
22:6; Deuteronomy 6:1–9

MAIN IDEA
Children are a blessing
from God and parents
are responsible for their
spiritual instruction.

QUESTION TO EXPLORE
What am I teaching
my children?

STUDY AIM
To thank God for my children
and to evaluate what I am
teaching my children

QUICK READ
Children are a blessing
from God. As parents, we
are responsible for their
nurture and instruction.

LESSON FOUR
Children

Introduction

Our daughter's birth was a memorable occasion for us. She is our oldest child and she arrived via an emergency C-section. We were in the labor and delivery room when various machines began to sound alarms. The nurses informed me that the doctor would arrive shortly and would decide the best course of action. He entered the room and assessed the situation. They had lost our daughter's heartbeat on the monitor. He looked at me and said, "We are already sedating Cindy. I'm not sure what is going on, but I am about to do an emergency C-section and find out. You stay here; I'll be right back with your baby."

With that, they wheeled Cindy out of the room and left me alone in a chair in the labor and delivery room. I had never felt so alone. We had family and friends in the waiting room, but I didn't dare move. About ten minutes later, the nurse walked toward me smiling and handed me our daughter. She was crying—and very much alive. "Your wife is fine," the nurse said. "She will be unconscious for about four hours. We will let you tell her she had a little girl."

I sat there with our little Hannah in my arms and thanked God. Our dream had come true. We were parents. A life-long journey had begun.

PSALM 127:3–5

[3] Sons are a heritage from the LORD,
   children a reward from him.
[4] Like arrows in the hands of a warrior
   are sons born in one's youth.
[5] Blessed is the man
   whose quiver is full of them.
 They will not be put to shame
   when they contend with their enemies in the gate.

PROVERBS 22:6

[6] Train a child in the way he should go, and when he is old he will not turn from it.

DEUTERONOMY 6:1–9

[1] These are the commands, decrees and laws the LORD your God directed me to teach you to observe in the land that you are crossing the Jordan to possess, [2] so that you, your children and their children after them may fear the LORD your God as long as you live by keeping all his decrees and commands that I give you, and so that you may enjoy long life. [3] Hear, O Israel, and be careful to obey so that it may go well with you and that you may increase greatly in a land flowing with milk and honey, just as the LORD, the God of your fathers, promised you.

[4] Hear, O Israel: The LORD our God, the LORD is one. [5] Love the LORD your God with all your heart and with all your soul and with all your strength. [6] These commandments that I give you today are to be upon your hearts. [7] Impress them on your children. Talk about them when you sit at home and when you walk along the road, when you lie down and when you get up. [8] Tie them as symbols on your hands and bind them on your foreheads. [9] Write them on the doorframes of your houses and on your gates.

Thankful For Our Children (Psalm 127:3–5)

The event I described occurred twenty-seven years ago. Our daughter is now happily married and has just delivered our first granddaughter. We are so excited to welcome a new generation into our family. However, we are still Hannah's parents. We still experience a sense of responsibility to assist Hannah in her spiritual development. We still pray for her and with her. We still talk with her about the lessons God is teaching us as adults. Our journey as parents continues even though she is a parent herself.

Parenting is a life-long journey. We don't graduate from it when our children graduate from high school. Even as adults, our children navigate through all types of challenges and difficult situations, and we as parents should be present and involved so we can offer guidance and counsel. We can share wisdom with them when they face life's inevitable setbacks. Parents play a unique role in their children's lives, no matter the age of the parent or the child.

Psalm 127 contains a positive perspective on parenting. The psalmist declared children to be a "heritage" and a "reward." Sons were particularly valued in ancient Israel because it was a patriarchal society. Men were the acknowledged leaders in the culture. Thus, "sons" were singled out in verse 3 before the psalmist expanded the blessing to include children of both genders.

In verses 4–5, the psalmist offered an image to help Israel understand the blessing of parenthood. Israel lived in a constant state of battle-readiness because of numerous threats around them. They were familiar with the equipment of war. Knowing this, the psalmist borrowed a war image—arrows in the hands of an accomplished warrior. Having sons was like being prepared for battle. Sons were viewed as security for the future. They could inherit the land and advance their father's name into the future. They were like arrows shot into the future.

In verse 5, the psalmist mentioned another ancient image. The elders of the city held court by the city gates. A man's son could represent the family at court proceedings. If an aging man had godly sons, he would never need to worry about them embarrassing him as they represented him and his interests. At the heart of Psalm 127:3–5 is the idea that God has chosen to bless families by providing children. Parents are to be thankful to God for their children.

Responsible For Our Children (Proverbs 22:6)

Proverbs 22:6 is often quoted in both Jewish and Christian circles. Many parents have relied on this verse when their children have strayed from the Christian worldview taught and modeled for them. Unfortunately, many parents have endured a fair amount of guilt when their adult children wander from the faith or leave the church. Parents have considered this verse to be a judgment of their parenting. They think that if they had trained their children properly, then their children would not have rejected the faith of their parents.

Believers need to consider this proverb contextually to properly apply its meaning. Ancient Israel was not a democratic republic that prized individualism. Our culture is very different. Children in ancient Israel were born into families with identities and roles that were accepted and valued. Farmers, shepherds, carpenters, fishermen, peasants, and vineyard keepers (and many more occupations) characterized the societal structures at the time. Children normally followed in the footsteps of their parents. A farmer in the hills of Nazareth would not need to teach his son the same skills as a fisherman who lived in Galilee. One would expect the farmer's son to adopt the life of a farmer in adulthood. It was the normal course of affairs in ancient Israel.

Consequently, we should begin with a common sense approach to this text. However, Jews and Christians have interpreted this text to apply to spiritual instruction as well. In other words, parents have the responsibility to provide spiritual instruction for their children. Parents are to both teach and model a life that honors God. The hope is that the children would grow to be righteous people as well. This proverb indicates that this is a *likely* outcome, not a guarantee.

This text doesn't offer carte blanche assurances that children will never stray from the way of the righteous. Although my parents raised

CHILD DEDICATION

"Train a child" from Proverbs 22:6 also carries the connotation of "dedication" as a part of its meaning. It presents the idea that parents should dedicate their children to the Lord. For example, Hannah dedicated Samuel to the Lord (1 Samuel 1:21–28). Although she left him with Eli the priest, Hannah continued to serve him as his mother. Dedicating children was common among the Jews, but leaving a child with a priest was not an everyday occurrence.

Mary and Joseph took Jesus to the temple to dedicate him to the Lord (Luke 2:22–24). This dedication was a solemn time of acknowledging God's blessing. During this time, parents would offer sacrifices to God, and then they would present their child to the Lord. Dedication was an expression of both gratitude and commitment on behalf of the parents. Today, believers practice a form of this ancient rite when parents dedicate their children in the local church. The parents present their children to the Lord and offer a commitment before God's people. Although a symbolic gesture with ancient roots, it still retains its contemporary relevance today.

my siblings and me in the core elements of the Christian faith, one of my siblings left the church and never returned. This caused great heartache and guilt for my parents. Yet, two brothers and I have served as pastors in local churches. We were all reared by the same parents. The principle of Proverbs 22:6 proved itself true in our family, but it does not apply universally to every situation or every family.

Impressing Truth Upon Our Children (Deuteronomy 6:1–9)

Any discussion about the biblical perspective on parenting must include Deuteronomy 6:1–9. This passage is a foundational text for God's people. The setting is during the final preparations prior to entering the Promised Land. Moses offered his final instructions. Israel was about to inherit the land God promised to the patriarchs. Moses wanted to insure the people remained committed to their God and his ways, so he reiterated the importance of following the commandments of God.

In the first two verses, Moses reminded the people that God expected obedience to his law. He had redeemed the Israelites from Egypt so they could inherit the land and prosper. God had already given his law to Israel at Mt. Sinai. Now on the plains of Moab, Moses re-emphasized God's expectations of Israel as a people.

Verses 4–5 were foundational to the people of Israel. This passage begins a section of the Law that Jews call the *Shema* (the Hebrew word for "hear"). To this day, Jews recite this passage as a prayer to God (along with Deuteronomy 11:13–21 and Numbers 15:37–41). It is a declaration of Israel's fundamental belief: The LORD (Yahweh) our God, the LORD is one. This statement is a powerful declaration of monotheism. This statement was also a declaration of the allegiance of the people. God was the sole object of their allegiance. The people demonstrated this truth by loving God with their whole heart, soul, and strength. Yahweh (translated LORD in English) is the covenantal name of the God of Israel (see Exodus 3). He called the nation to a deeply binding relationship (covenant) expressed in love and devotion. He singled out Israel from all the peoples of the world to represent him and his interests (Exod. 19:3–6).

Moses exhorted parents to be faithful to "impress" these foundational truths upon their children (Deut. 6:6–7). The parents' covenant

LIVING OUT THE SCRIPTURE

To live out the truths of this week's Scripture passage, consider putting into practice the following suggestions:

1. Pray for parents and children in your church.

2. Include children in worship and Bible study, as well as the overall life of the church. Include them in worship, fellowship, and instruction, all of which support parents in the spiritual formation of their children.

3. If you have not done so before, participate in your church's special time of dedication, during which you can present your children and yourself to the Lord.

4. If you are an empty nester, consider adopting a young couple to help nurture them as parents.

5. If your children are teens, talk with them about how your family can honor Christ in the home.

relationship with the only true God was to be on their hearts continually and was to be passed on to the next generation. Moses commanded the people to share the joy of knowing Yahweh as they went about the normal rhythms of life (sitting at home, walking along the way, lying down at night, etc.).

Parents must not assume that children inherently know these truths. Parents must be intentional about teaching them. In fact, Moses challenged the people to wear the teachings on their foreheads and hands, and to write the commands inside their homes. Scholars disagree as to whether God intended the Jews to actually "wear" these truths on their persons. Even today, some Jewish people wear phylacteries, which are small boxes that contain the law of God.

Clearly, God wanted his word to be in the thoughts (forehead) and in the actions (hands) of his people always. No matter life's events, children need parental instruction in the ways of God. Parents are the primary teachers of spiritual truth to their children, not the church. Today, parents need to be resourceful and creative in communicating spiritual truths to their children. We need to find ways to instruct our children throughout our family routines, taking advantage of teachable moments as they arise. Meal time, prayer time, recreation time, and travel time all provide excellent opportunities to relay spiritual truth to our children.

Implication and Actions

Children are a blessing from God, and he has made it clear that parents are responsible for raising their children. Parents are to take seriously the challenge of nurturing and training children to be godly followers of Jesus. In order to fulfill this task, parents must first maintain a vital walk with God themselves. We cannot model a godly lifestyle if we are not making time available for God to speak to us. From that primary relationship in a parent's life, children can hear and see the truth lived out in everyday life. This journey of encouragement and instruction extends to adult children and grandchildren. While we must be careful not to hover over our adult children too closely, we still can assist them in navigating the demands of their lives. Our grandchildren can also gain much from the godly examples of their grandparents.

QUESTIONS

1. How did your parents teach you about important life matters?

2. How are you teaching your children (regardless of their age) about faith in Christ?

3. Why is it important to view your children as a blessing from God?

4. What are some healthy ways parents can connect to adult children and grandchildren?

5. What are some things you wish you had done differently in passing along a life of faith to your children?

6. What have you learned (whether good or bad) from your parents' faith example?

LESSON FIVE
Parents

FOCAL TEXT
Exodus 20:12;
Luke 2:45–52; John 19:25–27

BACKGROUND
Exodus 20:1–21;
Luke 2:41–52; John 19:16–27

MAIN IDEA
Children are to love and
honor their parents.

QUESTION TO EXPLORE
How do I express love and
honor to my parents?

STUDY AIM
To consider how I can express
love and honor to my parents

QUICK READ
God commands us to love
and honor our parents. Jesus'
example, both as a child and
an adult, shows us how to
love and honor our parents.

Introduction

When my mother retired from her decades-long job, she already had new work waiting for her—caring for her elderly parents. Circumstances allowed her to move into her parents' home. Initially she helped them with shopping, meal preparation, cleaning, and yard work. Eventually, she drove both of them to doctors' appointments and helped them write checks to pay monthly bills. After my grandfather's death, my grandmother's health continued to deteriorate. In a role reversal, my mother acted as her mother's mother. My mother fed my grandmother, bathed her, dressed her, and gave her medicine. She allowed my grandmother to die with dignity in her own home. My mother loved and honored her parents by meeting their needs when they no longer could care for themselves.

Not every person can do what my mother did, but God calls all of us to honor our fathers and mothers. This applies to children of all ages and parents of any age. How are you expressing love and honor to your parents?[1]

EXODUS 20:12

[12] Honor your father and your mother, so that you may live long in the land the LORD your God is giving you.

LUKE 2:45–52

[45] When they did not find him, they went back to Jerusalem to look for him. [46] After three days they found him in the temple courts, sitting among the teachers, listening to them and asking them questions. [47] Everyone who heard him was amazed at his understanding and his answers. [48] When his parents saw him, they were astonished. His mother said to him, "Son, why have you treated us like this? Your father and I have been anxiously searching for you."

[49] "Why were you searching for me?" he asked. "Didn't you know I had to be in my Father's house?" [50] But they did not understand what he was saying to them.

51 Then he went down to Nazareth with them and was obedient to them. But his mother treasured all these things in her heart. 52 And Jesus grew in wisdom and stature, and in favor with God and men.

JOHN 19:25–27

25 Near the cross of Jesus stood his mother, his mother's sister, Mary the wife of Clopas, and Mary Magdalene. 26 When Jesus saw his mother there, and the disciple whom he loved standing nearby, he said to his mother, "Dear woman, here is your son," 27 and to the disciple, "Here is your mother." From that time on, this disciple took her into his home.

God's Command: How to Treat Parents (Exodus 20:12)

Jesus reduced all of the Old Testament laws to two commands: love God with all your being and love your neighbor as yourself (Matthew 22:34–40). The Ten Commandments reflect these two most important commandments. The first four address our relationship with God, while the last six guide our relationship with others, beginning with our parents. (See Sidebar: The Ten Words)

The fifth commandment, *honor your father and your mother*, applies to one of the most important human relationships. God instructs children how to treat their parents. *Honor* includes the ideas of giving weight to, glorifying, and esteeming. When we give our parents the honor that God commands, we value and appreciate them. We give our parents priority and take them seriously. We respect them. We care for them. We love them and demonstrate love through our actions. God's command gives equal status to mothers and fathers. Both parents should receive honor from their children.

In the Old Testament era, showing disrespect for one's parents was a serious crime in the covenant community. God gave the Israelites laws that made death the punishment for those who attacked or cursed their father or mother (Exodus 21:15, 17). Stubborn, rebellious children who disobeyed their parents and refused any discipline could be stoned to death (Deuteronomy 21:18–21).

The fifth commandment contains a promise: *that your days may be prolonged in the land which the LORD your God gives you.* Obviously, a lack of respect for parents in Old Testament times meant an abrupt end to life by capital punishment. This promise also pointed to the Israelites' tenure in the land of Canaan. The prophet Ezekiel declared that the failure to respect parents contributed to God scattering his people in exile (Ezekiel 22:7, 15).

Even for Christians today, this promise seems to have a community-focused meaning and does not necessarily mean a long life for every person. Families in which children honor and respect their parents make for strong communities and stable nations. Disrespect of parents leads to broken families and eventually to decaying communities where crime and violence often result in shortened life spans.

Although the fifth command applies to children of all ages, many Bible scholars emphasize its meaning for adult children. Grown children should take care of and provide for their aging parents when they are no

THE TEN WORDS

After delivering the Israelites from slavery in Egypt, God brought the people to Mt. Sinai where he established his covenant with them. He promised to make them his treasured possession, a kingdom of priests, and a holy nation if they obeyed his voice (Exod. 19:5–6). He had acted on their behalf. Now he required certain conduct from the people as their part of the agreement. He gave them Ten Words as principles for living in covenant relationship with the Lord their God.

What the Hebrew people called the Ten Words we identify as the Ten Commandments (see Exod. 34:28) or the *Decalogue.* This word comes from the Greek meaning *"ten words."* We find these commands in Exodus 20 and Deuteronomy 5.

The Ten Words provided the heart of the covenant relationship between God and the Israelites. These commandments also apply to those of us who have been adopted into God's family through our relationship with his Son.

longer able to work and care for themselves. Since children could easily neglect this duty, God insisted on this responsibility. Jesus criticized the religious leaders of his day who tried to justify not caring for their parents (Matt. 15:3–9).

Recently a friend shared that she and her husband were meeting with couples at their church who were entering a new phase of life—providing care for their senior parents. My friend has years of experience helping her aging parents. In speaking about their mentoring experiences, she said, "These couples aren't happy. They don't want to honor their parents because it takes a toll on their personal time." This honest statement reflects the struggle that some adult children undergo in seeking to honor their aging parents. Doing so may mean the sacrifice of time and resources. It may mean inconvenience, frustration, and changing plans. It may involve helping elderly parents maintain some control over their lives as long as possible, and not making all the decisions for them unless the need arises. Both children and parents will have to work out these personal matters together with the Lord's help.

Jesus' Example: How a Child Treats Parents (Luke 2:45–52)

The New Testament provides two events from Jesus' life in which he demonstrated how to treat one's parents. The first of these occurred when he was twelve-years-old. As devout Jews, Mary and Joseph traveled to Jerusalem every year to observe the Feast of the Passover, the first day of the Feast of Unleavened Bread. The Law required Jewish men to go to Jerusalem (if possible) to celebrate three great annual feasts—Passover, Pentecost, and Tabernacles. Distance kept many from participating in the feasts, but most Jews made an effort to journey to the city for the most significant of the three feasts—Passover. Passover recalled God's deliverance of his people from Egyptian slavery. The firstborn of the Egyptians died, but the Lord *passed over* the homes of the Hebrews who had smeared the blood of the sacrificial lamb on the doorposts of their homes (Exod. 12:1–39).

Jesus made the pilgrimage for Passover with Mary and Joseph when he was twelve-years-old. That Scripture records this particular pilgrimage does not rule out the possibility that he had gone with his parents to previous Passovers. The Jews believed a boy became a man at age thirteen

CASE STUDY

In August 2003, an intense heat wave sent temperatures soaring in France. Over 10,000 elderly people died of heat-related causes because their families, as well as health care workers and government officials, had gone on long vacations. They left these elderly adults alone with no help or air conditioning.

What causes people to neglect the needs of their aging parents? How does our culture contribute to the problem of neglecting the elderly? How can children take care of their maturing parents? What are your expectations of your children for your future care?

when he became a "son of the law" (or covenant) with new responsibility for keeping the law. At least two years before this event, boys would participate in the festivals in order to understand their future duties. Perhaps this trip to Jerusalem provided such a learning opportunity for Jesus.

The trip involved a two-day stay for the pilgrims at Passover. After this period, Mary and Joseph started the return trip to Nazareth, unaware that Jesus had remained behind in Jerusalem. For safety, extended families and neighbors traveled together in a caravan. At his age, Jesus could have walked with the women and younger children at the front of the group or with the men and older boys at the back of the caravan. Evidently Mary and Joseph thought he was with the other parent or others in the group. Only when they stopped to camp for the night did they realize his absence.

Mary and Joseph returned to Jerusalem to look for Jesus. They had traveled twenty to twenty-five miles from Jerusalem on the first day, and now they trekked back on day two. On the third day, they searched in the city for their son and finally found him in the temple with the religious teachers. The temple courts served as a place for teaching and learning. Jesus was both listening to the teachers and asking them questions. This question-and-answer session amazed those who heard it because of the depth of Jesus' answers and his spiritual understanding. Even Mary and Joseph wondered at Jesus' religious interest and insight.

Like any anxious parent, Mary exclaimed to Jesus, *"Son, why have you treated us like this?"* She reported how Joseph and she had been *anxiously* looking for him. The word denotes suffering and pain. They had been frantic with fear and worry.

Jesus' response reveals his understanding of his unique relationship with God, his Heavenly Father. He *had* to be in his Father's house. The word *had* implied strong moral necessity. Despite the miraculous events surrounding his birth twelve years earlier, his earthly parents still did not understand their special child.

Although Jesus recognized his greater loyalty to God, he returned to Jerusalem with Joseph and Mary. As one who always obeyed God, he was obedient to his earthly mother and father. In doing so, Jesus expressed love and honor to his parents. He continued to grow as a normal child—mentally, physically, spiritually, and socially.

When I ask first and second graders how they can obey God, usually one or more of them answers, "By obeying our parents." Children obey God by obeying their parents (Ephesians 6:1). Obedience is one way to show love and respect to mothers and fathers. If Jesus, the Son of God, obeyed his earthly parents, how much more should we obey our parents?

Jesus' Example: How an Adult Treats Parents (John 19:25–27)

At his crucifixion, Jesus gave another example of how adults should treat their aging parents. Despite his terrible suffering, Jesus fulfilled his duty as the eldest son to take care of his mother.

The Roman governor Pilate delivered Jesus over to a group of soldiers to be crucified. The four soldiers in charge of the execution divided Jesus' outer clothing among them. In fulfillment of Scripture (Psalm 22:18), they gambled for possession of Jesus' undergarment or tunic. In contrast to these cold-hearted men, some women also stood by the cross. Jesus' mother Mary, Mary's sister (probably named Salome), Mary the wife of Clopas, and Mary Magdalene all remained on the hill that day. These women loved and believed in Jesus. Neither their grief and distress nor the shame and humiliation at Jesus' death on the cross would cause them to abandon him.

Jesus saw his mother and John, *the disciple whom he loved*, at the foot of the cross. He asked John to take care of Mary as if she were his own mother. He asked Mary to recognize John as her son who would provide for her. From that moment, John took on the responsibility of protecting and providing for her. Although Jesus addressed Mary as "woman," this was a form of polite address in the first century. It sounds disrespectful to us, but it was not. Instead, Jesus loved and honored his mother even as his death approached. He put her needs above his own. He was intentional about providing care for her. We can follow his example.

Applying This Lesson to Life

In our self-focused society, we tend to dismiss the fifth commandment as applying more to young children than adult children. Many of us do not want our lives interrupted by caring for parents who once cared and sacrificed for us. Rearranging our schedules and priorities is costly and difficult. Yet, God's command and Jesus' example make clear our responsibility to care for our parents. The Apostle Paul declared that those who do not take care of their family members deny the faith and are worse than unbelievers (1 Timothy 5:8).

How do we love and honor our parents? For some, doing so may mean trying to mend a broken relationship by apologizing or forgiving. For young adults, it may mean sending regular text messages to keep parents informed. For median adults, it may involve a daily phone call to check on an aged parent or even including parents in family activities. For others, caring for parents may mean providing a home or assisted living for a parent who needs help. Living out this command will differ for each person, but the duty to show compassion and respect remains the same. How will you express love and honor to your mother and father?

QUESTIONS

1. How does children's obedience to parents contribute to the stability of society?

2. What should children do when obedience to parents directly contradicts God's commands? At what age should children stop obeying their parents?

3. How does a person express love and honor to parents when that relationship is strained by ongoing conflict and hurt?

4. How does Jesus' act of caring for his mother's needs challenge you in your relationship with your parents?

5. Look at the level of love and honor you are expressing to your parents. How would you evaluate your efforts? Do you need to make any changes?

6. Describe a time when you struggled to demonstrate respect and love to your parents. How did you resolve the conflict?

NOTES ————————————————————————————————

1. Unless otherwise indicated, all Scripture quotations in lessons 5–7 are from the New American Standard Bible (1995 edition).

LESSON SIX
Friends

Introduction

A man donates a kidney to a friend of thirty years. A soldier risks enemy fire to pull a fallen comrade to safety. A woman organizes a fundraiser for a neighbor victimized by a house fire. Friends help each other. I recall a time when a college friend drove with me three hours (and back) to another city on a Saturday so that I would not have to go to a job interview by myself. Two friends from my car-less seminary days never hesitated to let me borrow their vehicles. A church friend came immediately to take care of our four-year-old daughter when my husband had to rush me to the emergency room. God has given me loyal friends.

Loyalty means giving or showing firm, constant support to a person. Loyal friends are faithful, devoted, dependable, and unwavering. They keep confidences. They are interested in our well-being. They put our interests above their own. The Old Testament illustrates the value and rarity of a loyal friend in the relationship between David and Jonathan. Let's learn from their example.

ECCLESIASTES 4:9–12

9 Two are better than one,
   because they have a good return for their work:
10 If one falls down,
   his friend can help him up.
 But pity the man who falls
   and has no one to help him up!
11 Also, if two lie down together, they will keep warm.
   But how can one keep warm alone?
12 Though one may be overpowered,
   two can defend themselves.
 A cord of three strands is not quickly broken.

1 SAMUEL 20:1–17, 27–42

1 Then David fled from Naioth at Ramah and went to Jonathan and asked, "What have I done? What is my crime? How have I

wronged your father, that he is trying to take my life?"

[2] "Never!" Jonathan replied. "You are not going to die! Look, my father doesn't do anything, great or small, without confiding in me. Why would he hide this from me? It's not so!"

[3] But David took an oath and said, "Your father knows very well that I have found favor in your eyes, and he has said to himself, 'Jonathan must not know this or he will be grieved.' Yet as surely as the LORD lives and as you live, there is only a step between me and death."

[4] Jonathan said to David, "Whatever you want me to do, I'll do for you."

[5] So David said, "Look, tomorrow is the New Moon festival, and I am supposed to dine with the king; but let me go and hide in the field until the evening of the day after tomorrow. [6] If your father misses me at all, tell him, 'David earnestly asked my permission to hurry to Bethlehem, his hometown, because an annual sacrifice is being made there for his whole clan.' [7] If he says, 'Very well,' then your servant is safe. But if he loses his temper, you can be sure that he is determined to harm me. [8] As for you, show kindness to your servant, for you have brought him into a covenant with you before the LORD. If I am guilty, then kill me yourself! Why hand me over to your father?"

[9] "Never!" Jonathan said. "If I had the least inkling that my father was determined to harm you, wouldn't I tell you?"

[10] David asked, "Who will tell me if your father answers you harshly?"

[11] "Come," Jonathan said, "let's go out into the field." So they went there together.

[12] Then Jonathan said to David: "By the LORD, the God of Israel, I will surely sound out my father by this time the day after tomorrow! If he is favorably disposed toward you, will I not send you word and let you know? [13] But if my father is inclined to harm you, may the LORD deal with me, be it ever so severely, if I do not let you know and send you away safely. May the LORD be with you as he has been with my father. [14] But show me unfailing kindness like that of the LORD as long as I live, so that I may not be killed,

[15] and do not ever cut off your kindness from my family—not even when the LORD has cut off every one of David's enemies from the face of the earth."

[16] So Jonathan made a covenant with the house of David, saying, "May the LORD call David's enemies to account." [17] And Jonathan had David reaffirm his oath out of love for him, because he loved him as he loved himself.

• •

[27] But the next day, the second day of the month, David's place was empty again. Then Saul said to his son Jonathan, "Why hasn't the son of Jesse come to the meal, either yesterday or today?"

[28] Jonathan answered, "David earnestly asked me for permission to go to Bethlehem. [29] He said, 'Let me go, because our family is observing a sacrifice in the town and my brother has ordered me to be there. If I have found favor in your eyes, let me get away to see my brothers.' That is why he has not come to the king's table."

[30] Saul's anger flared up at Jonathan and he said to him, "You son of a perverse and rebellious woman! Don't I know that you have sided with the son of Jesse to your own shame and to the shame of the mother who bore you? [31] As long as the son of Jesse lives on this earth, neither you nor your kingdom will be established. Now send and bring him to me, for he must die!"

[32] "Why should he be put to death? What has he done?" Jonathan asked his father. [33] But Saul hurled his spear at him to kill him. Then Jonathan knew that his father intended to kill David.

[34] Jonathan got up from the table in fierce anger; on that second day of the month he did not eat, because he was grieved at his father's shameful treatment of David.

[35] In the morning Jonathan went out to the field for his meeting with David. He had a small boy with him, [36] and he said to the boy, "Run and find the arrows I shoot." As the boy ran, he shot an arrow beyond him. [37] When the boy came to the place where Jonathan's arrow had fallen, Jonathan called out after him, "Isn't the arrow beyond you?" [38] Then he shouted, "Hurry! Go quickly! Don't stop!" The boy picked up the arrow and returned to his

master. [39] (The boy knew nothing of all this; only Jonathan and David knew.) [40] Then Jonathan gave his weapons to the boy and said, "Go, carry them back to town."

[41] After the boy had gone, David got up from the south side [of the stone] and bowed down before Jonathan three times, with his face to the ground. Then they kissed each other and wept together—but David wept the most.

[42] Jonathan said to David, "Go in peace, for we have sworn friendship with each other in the name of the LORD, saying, 'The LORD is witness between you and me, and between your descendants and my descendants forever.'" Then David left, and Jonathan went back to the town.

Friendships Have Advantages (Ecclesiastes 4:9–12)

Ecclesiastes belongs to the wisdom literature of the Bible—those writings that help people deal with the practical and philosophical matters of life. Its writer called himself the Preacher (or Teacher), the son of David, king in Jerusalem (Ecclesiastes 1:1). Many biblical scholars identify him as Solomon. He wrote Ecclesiastes to help others learn an important truth from his personal experiences: only seeking God brings fulfillment and happiness.

The Preacher described as foolish the efforts of people who are completely alone without family or friends. Such individuals work to make more money, yet they are never satisfied with their wealth. Without children, they have no one to give all they have earned as an inheritance. They do not allow themselves to enjoy life (Eccles. 4:7–8).

In contrast to this gloomy picture of a solitary person, the Preacher presented a vital principle of companionship: *two are better than one* (4:9). The background of these advantages may refer to the difficult experience of traveling alone in Old Testament times. Solomon also commented on the benefits of loyal friendships. The first advantage involves having *a good return for their labor*. Working together—cooperation—has value and reward. When two people work together, they get more work done and help each other succeed. For example, my daughter helped her best friend address her wedding invitations. Their teamwork got the job done quickly. Friends working together make any task easier, faster, and more enjoyable.

The second benefit of friendship is having help in times of need. The Preacher pictured a person who falls down. After falling down, his companion helps him up (4:10). This value, however, has a wider application than physically falling. Whenever people have a crisis in their lives, they often call their friends even before family members. Loyal friends will make themselves available to help in times of distress or personal struggles. In a way, those friends lift up their struggling companion.

The third benefit involves sharing resources. In Bible times, travelers often slept on the ground in cold night temperatures. Two traveling companions who shared a blanket or other covering multiplied their body heat and thus provided warmth for each other (4:11). Perhaps this advantage applies today as we share our resources with friends in need. For instance, in our mission congregation, many of us provide transportation for those members who have car problems. Friends share tools, books, dishes, food, money, and countless other resources as a demonstration of loyal kinship.

NEW MOON

The Israelites set aside for worship the first day of each lunar month—the day of the new moon. This celebration allowed the people to dedicate the coming month to the LORD. Pagan nations held festivals during the full moon and worshipped the moon itself. In contrast, the Israelites held their festivities at the new moon—when the moon could not be seen. This act kept them from worshipping the creation instead of the Creator. At times, the festival was celebrated for two days due to the difficulty of determining the exact day of the new moon.

The new moon ceremonies were similar to those of the Sabbath but possessed an element of joy, with no fasting or mourning. Like the Sabbath, people ceased from work. The celebration included feasting, offering of sacrifices, and the blowing of trumpets. Numbers 28:11–15 describes the offerings for the new moon. These were greater in quantity and quality than those for the Sabbath. The new moon festival was still observed in New Testament times (Colossians 2:16).

A final advantage shared by friends is protection. Again, this likely refers to the dangerous travel conditions of the ancient world. Two companions would be better able to defend themselves against an attack and hold their ground. An opponent could easily overpower a person who is alone (4:12). Although most of our friends today would not have to protect us physically, they may have to defend our actions or character. Additionally, friends can remind us of our faith and trust in God when the devil—the ultimate enemy of all believers—attacks us.

The Preacher used a proverb to emphasize these assets of companionship. One cannot easily tear apart a three-stranded rope (4:12). It has strength and power. Weakness comes from working alone.

In a healthy relationship, these friendship benefits are mutually offered and exchanged. These advantages result when friends are willing to share themselves and their resources with each other. Loyal friendship develops as each person invests time, energy, and resources. What loyal friend has God given you?

Friends Help Each Other (1 Samuel 20:1–17)

The friendship between David and Jonathan, King Saul's son, exemplifies what it means to be a loyal friend. The two became friends after David killed the Philistine giant Goliath. They shared much in common—courage, skill as warriors, youth, cunning, and faith. They made a covenant with each other at the beginning of their friendship because of their mutual love (1 Samuel 18:3).

After David proved himself by defeating Goliath, Saul sent David out repeatedly to fight the Philistines. His successes and the resulting praise of the people made Saul jealous. He intended to kill David and made several attempts on his life. In one foiled attempted, he told Jonathan and all his servants to kill David. Jonathan showed loyalty to his friend by warning David. Then Jonathan convinced Saul of David's innocence and his helpfulness to the king (1 Sam. 19:1–7).

David decided he would have to flee from Saul. He came to Jonathan and asked him why his father wanted to kill him. Jonathan did not think Saul was trying to kill David because he believed his father told him everything he planned to do. David used several solemn oaths to convince Jonathan that because his father knew about their friendship, his

WHAT KIND OF FRIEND ARE YOU?

How would you evaluate yourself as a friend? Which of the following statements apply to you?

- I choose my friends based on how I can help them, not how they can help me.
- I desert my friends when they are having trouble and need my help.
- I am willing to help my friends even when doing so is inconvenient.
- I give up on my friends instead of working through our conflicts.
- I keep my friends' secrets.
- I gossip about my friends when they are not present.
- I forgive my friends when they hurt me.

What actions can you take to become a more loyal friend?

father would not tell Jonathan about wanting to kill David (20:3). Jonathan promised to help David: *Whatever you say, I will do for you* (20:4).

David formed a plan to determine Saul's intent toward him. He would not attend the new moon feast. Saul's reaction to David's absence would reveal his true attitude toward David. David reminded Jonathan that it was Jonathan's idea to make a *covenant of the LORD* with him (20:8), promising to be a loyal friend. David asked Jonathan himself to kill him if David had done anything wrong, preferring death by a friend rather than execution by an enemy.

Jonathan assured David he would find out if his father wanted to kill him. God would be the witness of his truthfulness. Jonathan repeatedly referred to the LORD or Yahweh, the covenant-making God, as he talked with his friend. He asked the LORD to punish him if he did not keep his promise to David. He also prayed that God would bless David even as he had previously blessed Saul.

Jonathan wanted David to promise that he would show kindness to Jonathan and his descendants when David had won victory over all his enemies and became king. This promise was important to Jonathan because in those days, kings often put to death the family and supporters of the previous ruler to get rid of potential rivals. David showed his faithfulness to keep this promise after Jonathan's death. He extended kindness to Jonathan's son Mephibosheth by providing a home for him (2 Sam. 9).

Jonathan made a plan to relay to David Saul's intention toward David. David would hide in a field. In two days, Jonathan would come to the same field and pretend to practice shooting arrows. The words he used to instruct his servant boy to retrieve the arrows would alert David to the answer. Interestingly, if David had to leave, Jonathan said the LORD has sent you away (1 Sam. 20:22). This underscores their trust in God to bless their friendship even when challenged by Jonathan's father.

As a result of their deep friendship, Jonathan helped David even though it meant great loss for Jonathan—the right to the throne. Jonathan betrayed his own father by affirming his loyalty to David. He was willing to risk physical safety and emotional turmoil to support his friend. What help are you willing to give your friends? Are you prepared to make sacrifices for them?

Friends Keep Promises (1 Samuel 20:27–42)

The two friends put their plan into action. David did not attend the new moon festival, although Saul expected his leaders' participation. (See Sidebar: New Moon.) On the first day of his absence, Saul thought that David was ceremonially unclean, disqualifying him from taking part in the feast. The king knew David's commitment to follow God's laws. When David failed to attend the festival on the second day, Saul questioned Jonathan to learn why the "son of Jesse" was absent (20:27). Interestingly, Saul refused to use his son-in-law's name, which was a way to insult him. As planned, Jonathan told how David had returned to Bethlehem for a family sacrifice.

Saul's reaction was swift. He was furious! David had chosen his family's celebration over that of a king! He directed his anger, complete with vulgar name-calling, toward Jonathan, insulting his mother—Saul's wife—and calling Jonathan a traitor. He reminded Jonathan that to support David meant forfeiting his own kingdom. He insisted that Jonathan bring David to him so that David could be killed.

When Jonathan defended David's innocence, Saul hurled his spear at him, trying to kill his own son because he had identified with David. Finally, Jonathan understood his father's murderous intentions toward his best friend. He left the table in fierce anger and could not eat. His father's insults and dishonor toward David grieved him. Jonathan was more worried about the just treatment of his friend than in securing the throne for himself, another sign of his loyalty to David. Deep, enduring friendships involve self-sacrifice.

According to plan, the next day Jonathan took a servant boy with him to target practice. Jonathan shot an arrow so that it would go beyond the child. He said to the servant, "Hurry, be quick, do not stay!" (20:38). These words sent a clear message to David—his life was in danger. When the boy retrieved the arrow, Jonathan sent him back to town with the bow and arrows. Meeting with David without weapons showed that Jonathan meant David no harm.

When David approached Jonathan, he bowed to the ground before him three times, showing his respect for his friend and Jonathan's superiority as future king. In keeping with Middle East tradition, the two men "kissed each other and wept" (20:41), just as Joseph kissed his brothers and wept (Genesis 45:14–15). As he sent his friend away, Jonathan reminded David of the covenant they had made to take care of each other's families. David departed and Jonathan returned to town. Apart from a brief encounter (1 Sam. 23:16–18), this was the last time David and Jonathan would see each other.

Jonathan demonstrated his loyalty to David by seeking his friend's well-being above his own. He showed sacrificial love. Neither man pursued any selfish gain from their relationship. Both men kept their promises to each other. How have you strengthened your relationships by your faithfulness?

Applying This Lesson to Life

Loyal friends are gifts from God. They help us get the job done. They support us in our times of trouble. They comfort us when we are hurting or when we face stressful situations. They protect us from our enemies.

Loyal friends help each other—even when doing so may not be convenient and even when it may be risky. Faithful friends keep promises to each other, never breaking a confidence or changing their minds. We prove that our friendship is genuine when we show faithfulness to our friends.

The friendship loyalty between Jonathan and David challenges each of us to examine our relationships. Do we put the needs and interests of our friends above our own? Are we willing to make personal sacrifices for our friends? Do we encourage each other's faith in God? Do we trust each other with our deepest thoughts and attitudes? Let's ask the Lord to help us to be loyal to our friends.

QUESTIONS

1. When have you put the needs of a friend above your personal well-being? What was the result? How did it strengthen your friendship? When has someone else put your needs first? How did it impact your relationship?

2. How does basing your friendship on commitment to God and not one another make it stronger and more intimate?

3. What characteristics of the relationship between Jonathan and David would you like to cultivate in your friendships?

4. In what ways does Jesus show that he is our loyal friend?

5. How would you respond to people who claim that the friendship between David and Jonathan was homosexual in nature?

FOCAL TEXT
Luke 6:27–36; Romans 12:17–21

BACKGROUND
Luke 6:27–36; Romans 12:9–21

MAIN IDEA
Christ followers are expected
to love their enemies.

QUESTION TO EXPLORE
How can we follow Jesus'
command to love our enemies?

STUDY AIM
To choose to follow Jesus'
command to love my enemies

QUICK READ
Jesus wants his followers
to love their enemies,
following God's example of
kindness and mercy, and
defeating evil with good.

LESSON SEVEN
Enemies

Introduction

At his annual performance review, Joan's husband Tom received several low evaluations. Tom's supervisor spoke insulting words to him. Tom knew he had done well in some of the criticized areas. He believed that management was trying to force him out of his job like former co-workers. As a result, Joan disliked Tom's boss and his treatment of her husband. She criticized the man repeatedly and believed he lacked integrity. Joan thought of this man as "the enemy."

One day when she read Jesus' words, "love your enemies . . . pray for those who mistreat you" (Luke 6:27–28), the Holy Spirit convicted Joan of her attitude toward Tom's boss. She began to pray for him. When the supervisor's wife asked for help with a community project, Joan volunteered to assist her. The Lord enabled Joan to act for the good of her "enemy."

Jesus Christ expects his followers to love their enemies. He calls us to a higher standard of conduct than unbelievers. Have we accepted this challenge?

LUKE 6:27–36

27 "But I tell you who hear me: Love your enemies, do good to those who hate you, 28 bless those who curse you, pray for those who mistreat you. 29 If someone strikes you on one cheek, turn to him the other also. If someone takes your cloak, do not stop him from taking your tunic. 30 Give to everyone who asks you, and if anyone takes what belongs to you, do not demand it back. 31 Do to others as you would have them do to you.

32 If you love those who love you, what credit is that to you? Even 'sinners' love those who love them. 33 And if you do good to those who are good to you, what credit is that to you? Even 'sinners' do that. 34 And if you lend to those from whom you expect repayment, what credit is that to you? Even 'sinners' lend to 'sinners,' expecting to be repaid in full. 35 But love your enemies, do good to them, and lend to them without expecting to get anything back. Then your reward will be great, and you will be sons of the Most High, because he is kind to the ungrateful and wicked. 36 Be merciful, just as your Father is merciful."

ROMANS 12:17–21

¹⁷ Do not repay anyone evil for evil. Be careful to do what is right in the eyes of everybody. ¹⁸ If it is possible, as far as it depends on you, live at peace with everyone. ¹⁹ Do not take revenge, my friends, but leave room for God's wrath, for it is written: "It is mine to avenge; I will repay," says the Lord. ²⁰ On the contrary:
"If your enemy is hungry, feed him;
    if he is thirsty, give him something to drink.
In doing this, you will heap burning coals on his head."
²¹ Do not be overcome by evil, but overcome evil with good.

Choose to Act in Love (Luke 6:27–31)

Jesus gave directions for his followers in what is called the Sermon on the Plain (Luke 6:20–49), a shorter version of the Sermon on the Mount (Matthew 5–7). In this sermon, he outlined how his followers should live in relationship with other people. Jesus began with a direct command: love your enemies (6:27). An enemy is a person who is actively opposed or hostile toward us. An enemy may hate us, threaten us, attempt to harm us in some way, or stop us from doing something.

Enemies seek our harm. They may injure or threaten us. We may think of enemies in broad terms. Americans viewed Osama bin Laden, the leader of al-Qaeda and instigator of the 9/11 attacks, as an enemy. In 2014, many Americans added the Islamic State (ISIS or ISIL) terrorist leader Abu Bakr al-Baghdadi to the list of enemies. However, we all have enemies who are more personal. Who threatens us—socially, economically, physically, spiritually? Who opposes us? Most of us can name someone who wounds us in some way.

Jesus commanded his followers to show *agape* (unconditional) love. *Agape* love for our enemies is not based on our feelings but on our will. We may not like those who have harmed us, but we can choose to act on their behalf. Our natural preference would be to hate and hurt our enemies. However, God wants us to be different from our sinful world. The Lord wants us to see all people (not a select few) as he sees them—in need of love and forgiveness. God's grace equips us to obey this demanding challenge to love the unlovely and those hostile to us, even if they never return the love or act in our interests. An adversary's response does not matter. Our obedience does.

Jesus gave three commands that outline how believers can choose to act in love. First, believers can do good to those who hate them (6:27). To love an enemy means doing good to, and taking positive action toward, people who do not offer good in return. Jesus' words must have shocked his first Jewish hearers. What? Do good to those cruel Romans who controlled their country? Yes! Even today, this command can incite a strong reaction. What? Do good to that person who hurts me? Yes!

Secondly, we as believers must bless those who curse us (6:28). *To bless* means to speak well of a person. We choose to act in love when we ask God to care for and provide good things for those who speak to us harshly or hope that bad things happen to us. We imitate God's grace when we choose to speak well of someone who has spoken badly of us.

Finally, we must pray for those who mistreat us (6:28). God can work through our prayers to not only change those who threaten us, but also to change our attitudes toward them. Prayer enables us to forgive and not strike back.

In verse 29, Jesus provided concrete examples of choosing to act in love in the face of persecution. In both instances—when someone hits our face and when someone steals our coat—Jesus encouraged us not to insist on our personal rights nor reciprocate with hostile acts. Despite the pain, the insult, and the material loss, we should do what is best for the evildoer. This means forgiving, denying our desire to retaliate, and putting aside our personal interests. However, acting in love does not mean we cannot defend ourselves in the face of deadly attack.

For emphasis, Jesus exaggerated the command in verse 30. He was not telling his followers to condone someone's bad choices to steal or cause physical harm. However, he was telling his listeners to respond in a radically different way. We should give generously and freely, thinking of others' needs and not clinging to our possessions. Even if robbed, we should think of the robber's situation. We should think of the demands made of us as coming from genuine need. We should be willing to forsake our own needs to help others, not expecting repayment. Jesus commanded us to treat other people exactly as we would like for them to treat us (6:31). (See sidebar: The Golden Rule.)

THE GOLDEN RULE

We call Luke 6:31 the "Golden Rule." Jesus affirmed that this statement sums up the moral teachings of the Law and the Prophets (Matthew 7:12). It defines the daily conduct expected of believers—treating others as they would like to be treated.

Parallels to the Golden Rule appeared in Greco-Roman, Eastern (Confucius, for example), and Jewish literature. Most—but not all—of those writers expressed the idea in a negative form. For instance, the first-century Rabbi Hillel quoted Tobit 4:15 (a book written between the Old and New Testaments): "What you do not wish done to you, do not to others." Rabbis commonly stressed this negatively worded statement.

In contrast, Jesus emphasized the positive, more demanding expression of this principle. The Lord's followers must do more than passively refrain from doing what they would not have done to themselves. Instead, they must take the initiative in doing what is good for others. They do to others the good they want for themselves despite the way people treat them.

How can we follow Jesus' command to love our enemies? We can choose to respond in love. We can determine to act kindly whether or not we feel like it. We can show grace whether or not we like our oppressors. We can demonstrate kindness whether or not we receive any benefit or kindness in return, and whether or not our foes continue to oppose us. We can choose to forgive.

Follow God's Example (Luke 6:32–36)

Jesus presented three illustrations demonstrating how his followers should surpass unbelievers in conduct—loving others who don't love in return; doing good to those who would cause us harm; and lending without expecting some return. He explained that loving others, doing good, and lending to those who already love us does not demonstrate God-like love. Unbelievers often operate under the principle of reciprocity—doing something for someone in order to receive a benefit. In contrast, *agape* love expects nothing in return. Consequently, we as God's people should love those who do not love us. We should do good to those who wrong us. We should lend without expecting anything back. Does this seem impossible to do? The power of the indwelling Spirit of God makes this possible. We can pray and ask for his help.

God promises a great reward (6:35) for those who make the choice to love their enemies and do good toward others. This reward is not a payment for good behavior. Rather, the mention of a reward simply illustrates God's blessing on those who obey him. This reward may be the comfort and peace of having done what is right before the Most High. It may be fellowship with our Heavenly Father and increased opportunities for service.

Our obedience to God does not make us his children. We do not earn our relationship with God when we choose to treat our enemies with love and mercy and grace. Rather, the reference to being "sons of the Most High" means that we will show ourselves to be his children. We prove that we are truly his by responding as he would (and did). Our actions should be dramatically different than actions of sinners because of the character of God himself. God is kind to the ungrateful and evil. As his children, we should reflect his nature. We too should show love and kindness to those who do not deserve it. God showed his love for us by sending Jesus Christ to die for us—while we were still sinners

PRAY FOR YOUR ENEMIES

- On a personal level, what relationships do you have that are strained by hostility or conflict? In your church or community, who has angered or hurt you? In your career, who opposes you, treats you unfairly, or tries to hurt you? Determine to pray for these individuals on a regular basis. Ask God for forgiveness, patience, understanding, and power to act in love toward these persons.

- On a broader scale, pray for those whose intent is to harm our country. For example, commit to praying for the Islamic State of Iraq and Syria (ISIS), other terrorists, and other radicals within our own borders who seek to bring about chaos and destruction.

(Romans 5:8). We should be merciful because our Father is merciful (Luke 6:36).

How can we follow Jesus' command to love our enemies? We can follow his example. We can imitate our Heavenly Father and reflect his character in our lives through loving, kind, and merciful attitudes and actions toward those who are hostile toward us.

Defeat Evil with Good (Romans 12:17–21)

In Romans 12, Paul's letter shifts from theological concepts to practical application, giving guidelines for how believers should live in a fallen world. Paul's teachings echo those from Jesus' Sermon on the Plain in Luke 6. In verses 14–21, the apostle especially targeted how Christ followers should act toward non-Christians.

Paul repeated Jesus' principle of non-retaliation (12:17). When people do wrong things to us, we should not do wrong things to them to get even. The word "anyone" means we do not retaliate against believers, unbelievers, Americans, Asians, Hispanics, gang members, Democrats, Republicans, Muslims, or atheists. It does not matter who commits the evil against us; we are not to seek revenge. We accept and absorb the injury, imitating Christ's actions on the cross.

Our public behavior should not discredit the gospel of Jesus Christ (12:17). Doing what is right "in the eyes of everybody" does not mean that believers should be people pleasers. Rather, Paul was challenging the believers to respond in such a way that our behavior is above reproach. When we live by our Lord's higher standards, nonbelievers notice. Our actions serve as a positive witness of the gospel to others.

Believers should also make every effort to live at peace with everyone (12:18). The phrase, "if it is possible" indicates that situations may arise in which peace is not possible despite our efforts as peacemakers. We cannot control other people's behavior. However, we should not be a part of the problem, as shown by the words "as far as it depends on you." At times, our stand for biblical truth may cause conflict. We should not sacrifice truth to maintain peace.

Love never takes revenge (12:19). We should trust God, casting on him our distress over being wronged. God knows the situation better than we do. We can let his wrath take care of the injustice instead of taking matters into our own hands. God will repay. He avenges the wronged and knows the appropriate punishment. Paul quoted Deuteronomy 32:35 to remind us that God is the Judge.

Instead of taking vengeance, we should help and meet the needs of our enemies (Rom. 12:20). Paul used the principle from Proverbs 25:21–22 to illustrate the point. The picture of heaping burning coals on our enemies' heads suggests shaming them. When we return kindness and forgiveness for wrongs suffered, our foes may see their sinful actions in stark contrast to God's love. This kindness could lead to remorse and cause them to repent. Love may change our enemies, making them our friends.

When we retaliate and return evil for evil, not only do we add to the wrongs committed, we allow evil to overcome us. We sink to the level of our enemies. Sin wins. Instead, Jesus wants us to defeat evil with good (Rom. 12:21), using the "weapons" of love, kindness, goodness, and forgiveness.

How can we follow Jesus' command to love our enemies? We can defeat evil with good by choosing not to retaliate.

Applying This Lesson to Life

We live in a culture and time in history when people often *demand* their real (or imagined) rights. The commands to love our enemies, do good to those who hate us, and to never pay back evil to anyone contradicts those claims of entitlement. As believers, we follow Christ's higher standard. We are not to copy the behavior and attitudes of the non-Christians around us. We are to imitate Jesus. He gives us the Holy Spirit's enabling grace and power to do those things that are not natural for us.

The next time someone wounds you, try forgiveness instead of retaliation. You may not *feel* like forgiving, but your forgiveness may lead to a new relationship. Letting go of the need to take revenge will free you from frustration and bitterness. The next time you experience hostility, respond with a kind action—help the person, pray for the person, or send a note or gift. Right feelings often follow right actions.

When I taught about loving our enemies to a group of children, one child exclaimed, "I don't want to do that!" I appreciated his honesty. Loving our enemies is a matter of our will. Will we choose to obey Jesus, even when it's difficult?

QUESTIONS

1. How can you "turn the other cheek" without passively accepting evil or failing to take legal actions when necessary?

2. Does love for our enemies eliminate the need for the military or weapons? Explain your answer.

3. What specific actions can you take to show love to someone in your life whom you find difficult?

4. How can following Jesus' instruction to love our enemies open the door to sharing Christ with them?

5. What would our community look like if everybody practiced non-retaliation?

FOCAL TEXT
Exodus 20:13–17;
Leviticus 19:16–18;
Zechariah 7:8–10;
Matthew 5:13–16

BACKGROUND
Exodus 20:13–17;
Leviticus 19:16–18;
Zechariah 7:8–10;
Matthew 5:13–16

MAIN IDEA
We are to respect, love,
and serve our neighbors
as a witness to our faith.

QUESTION TO EXPLORE
Do I respect, love, and
serve my neighbors as a
witness to my faith?

STUDY AIM
To consider how I can respect,
love, and serve my neighbors
as a witness to my faith

QUICK READ
The biblical mandate to
take the good news of Jesus
to the ends of the earth
begins at our doorstep. Our
first mission field is with
neighbors who need to
experience our positive faith.

LESSON EIGHT
Neighbors/ Community

Introduction

Most people live in "community" as individuals who share common values with others. That sense of community relates to all kinds of people—from thieves to friends—wherever people find common bonds that link them with others. Our focus on community will center on those who live nearby, our neighbors. We will view four passages of Scripture that cover a long period of Jewish-Christian history, from the Exodus to the time of Christ. As you study these passages, look for their rich meaning, but also consider how they illustrate ways to help people connect to one another and to God. The faith that we bring to the study of God's word can impact the lives of those who live near us.

EXODUS 20:13–17

13 "You shall not murder.

14 "You shall not commit adultery.

15 "You shall not steal.

16 "You shall not give false testimony against your neighbor.

17 "You shall not covet your neighbor's house. You shall not covet your neighbor's wife, or his manservant or maidservant, his ox or donkey, or anything that belongs to your neighbor."

LEVITICUS 19:16–18

16 "'Do not go about spreading slander among your people. 'Do not do anything that endangers your neighbor's life. I am the LORD.

17 "'Do not hate your brother in your heart. Rebuke your neighbor frankly so you will not share in his guilt.

18 "'Do not seek revenge or bear a grudge against one of your people, but love your neighbor as yourself. I am the LORD."

ZECHARIAH 7:8–10

8 And the word of the LORD came again to Zechariah: 9 "'This is what the LORD Almighty says: Administer true justice; show mercy

and compassion to one another. [10] Do not oppress the widow or the fatherless, the alien or the poor. In your hearts do not think evil of each other.'"

MATTHEW 5:13–16

[13] "You are the salt of the earth. But if the salt loses its saltiness, how can it be made salty again? It is no longer good for anything, except to be thrown out and trampled by men.

[14] "You are the light of the world. A city on a hill cannot be hidden. [15] Neither do people light a lamp and put it under a bowl. Instead they put it on its stand, and it gives light to everyone in the house. [16] In the same way, let your light shine before men, that they may see your good deeds and praise your Father in heaven.

Neighbors Practice the Basic Ten (Exodus 20:13–17)

The first word that many children learn is *no*. Parents are not being negative when they say *no* to their children; they are teaching them how to avoid things that harm them. Saying *no* actually reinforces behaviors that can be healthy and helpful. When we turn our attention to the Ten Commandments, some people see them as negatives, and that is understandable. Israel was in its infancy and toddler stages as a people of God. They needed to know what the boundaries were, what behavior was acceptable to God, and what was outside the boundaries.

The first four commandments deal with our relationship to God. We learn that God comes first, and we should have no substitutes for God. We should accept God's nature and purpose in earnest, and we should celebrate our relationship with him in worship. The next six commandments address our relationships with others, beginning with our relationship to our parents. We are commanded to honor them. We also are to live in ways that reveal God, as stated in commandments that focus on a range of sinful behaviors from murder to coveting. Jesus amplified our understanding of these in the Sermon on the Mount (Matthew 5–7), a section of Scripture that is useful for a deeper understanding of the Ten Commandments.

Murder is the premeditated and intentional taking of another person's life. Life is precious to God because people are created in the image of God (Genesis 1:26). Life has its accidents, wars, and exceptional circumstances; but almost every civilization has set forth prohibitions against, and punishments for, murder. Jesus extended this command by warning his listeners about hating someone, which is the catalyst that leads to the shedding of blood and murder (Matt. 5:21–27).

Adultery is a violation of the sacred nature of the marital relationship. Marriage and family relationships need to be encouraged and honored. In the Old Testament, Joseph understood that committing adultery with Potiphar's wife was not only a sin against her and her husband, but it was also a sin against God (Gen. 39). He knew not to cross that line, even though God had not given the Ten Commandments yet. Adultery also negates the covenant involving God, husband, and wife (Matt. 19:4–6).

Jesus warned that "committing adultery in your heart" (Matt. 5:27) through lustful looking is sinful. A long time ago, I asked a professor at Baylor University about what Jesus meant here, and the difference

COVENANT PEOPLE

Covenant is a central concept in biblical faith and Christian history. Some refer to the Bible as containing two parts, the Old Covenant and the New Covenant. The Old Testament contains many covenants, including God's covenants with Noah, Abraham, Moses, and David. Jeremiah pointed us to the New Covenant, which finds its fulfillment in Jesus. Church history records many historic covenants that underscore basic beliefs and practices of denominations or churches.

Commit yourself to being a "covenant person" with your neighbors. We will encounter one-sided covenants in which our neighbors are not equally committed to us. That should not deter us. Our neighborly covenant begins with God, and then extends to those who are affected by our commitment. As we treat others with the grace we receive from God, we enter into new covenants of respect, love, and service with those who live near us. Your commitment to being a covenant person with your neighbors will inspire and help others.

between some occasional fleeting thoughts and lustful looking. He answered, "You can't keep the birds from flying over your head, but you can keep them from making a nest in your hair." Then, running his hands through his gray hair, he said, "Even at my age, I have to brush away the birds away occasionally."

Next, God set forth the command against stealing. The psalmist viewed all possessions as ultimately belonging to God (Psalm 24:1), and that theology is part of the biblical teaching that we are managers and trustees on behalf of God. To steal something would violate that principle, and it would also lead to disruption in community life. In the New Testament, Paul wrote to new Christians who may not have been familiar with the ethic of the Ten Commandments. He wrote that the thief should no longer steal, but work so that he has something to share with others (Ephesians 4:28). God intended for us not to be takers, but workers and givers.

The Ten Commandments also address lying about a neighbor (someone with whom you have a relationship). Slander, gossip, and other verbal offenses destroy community. Christians should speak the "truth in love" (Eph. 4:15) and must "put off falsehood and speak truthfully to his neighbor" (Eph. 4:25). When we do so, we guard each other and our community from the problems of slanderous and false conversations that do not protect the good name of one's neighbor.

The first commandment (having no other gods) sets a believer's priority, putting God first (see Matt. 6:33). The last command has the advantage of finality, "do not covet." Jesus said, "Be on your guard against all kinds of greed" (Luke 12:15). The warning in Exodus 20:17 concerns coveting anything that relates to "your neighbor" but its application goes far beyond those who live nearby. Coveting anything from anyone can lead to a violation of all the commandments, and it can destroy our most important relationships.

The essence of the Christian faith is not distilled into a list of "thou shalt nots." However, that does not diminish the wisdom and power of the Ten Commandments. The Israelites needed them early in their experience with God because a covenant relationship with him was so new. As time passed, the Hebrew people found out that these foundational principles were not merely behaviors that were acceptable to God. The Ten Commandments expressed values to embrace and provided important directional markers about how their society should be structured in order for it to flourish and thrive.

Neighbors Love Neighbors (Leviticus 19:16–18)

Biblical scholars identify Leviticus 17—26 as "The Holiness Code." What do you think of when you read the word "holy?" Perhaps you envision the first section of the Ten Commandments, the first four commands that speak of your relationship with God. That instruction certainly is covered in the holiness code. However, when you read these chapters, the overwhelming portion of the holiness code relates to the second section of the Ten Commandments—how you relate to other people. Holiness is defined in part by your respect, treatment, and care for others. It is important in building healthy relationships with anyone, because love behaves in ways that reflect the goodness and holiness of God as well as genuine care for others.

Leviticus 19:16–18 concludes with one of the two great commandments that Jesus identified (Matt. 22:34–40). The first great commandment is to love God with all that you are, and the second is to love your neighbor as yourself. Though Jesus did not identify any of the Ten Commandments with the "great" label, these two verses sum up the two divisions of the Ten Commandments: our relationship to God and our relationship to others.

Pay attention to Leviticus 19:16: "Do not do anything that endangers your neighbor's life." Obviously, the forbidden behaviors in

---

WHO IS MY NEIGHBOR?

A lawyer raised a question to Jesus in response to Jesus' mention of the commandment "to love your neighbor as yourself" (Luke 10:29). The lawyer asked, "Who is my neighbor?" Jesus responded by telling the story of the Good Samaritan (Luke 10:30–37). The point of the story is that your neighbor is any person who needs help. That is broader than the focus of our study, because we are focusing on those who live nearby; however, Jesus' story is still appropriate. Do you really know your neighbors? Do you know anything about their needs? Do you even know their names? This week, make an intentional effort to build relationships with those living nearest to you (For more help see www.pray4everyhome.com.)

commandments 6–10, from murder to coveting, endanger your neighbor's life. However, verse 16 begins with a focus on our words—"do not go about spreading slander among your people." As children, we may have said, "Sticks and stones may break my bones, but words will never hurt me." We soon learned that rhyme is not true. Words can hurt and wound people. God's people, however, are to speak differently. Slander and false witness have no place among Christ followers.

The focus of application applies to those who live near us. We can begin with the commitment of not doing anything that endangers our neighbor, and that is good and honorable. However, doing so does not define the full intention of these verses or our Christian obligation. Sometimes, not all goes well in the neighborhood. What then? Do we love people enough to seek reconciliation, even rebuking, in order to experience a better community of neighbors? If we love without slander, hatred, revenge, gossip, or grudges, then we go a long way in building relationships. We reveal that we know what "love your neighbor as yourself" means.

Neighbors Do the Right Thing (Zechariah 7:8–10)

Zechariah was a religious leader who helped those returning from Babylonian exile to rebuild the temple in Jerusalem around 520 B.C. His passion was to see people genuinely live out their faith. Legalism and outward works with no inner change were not sufficient. Faith oriented toward God contains a moral fiber that grows out of genuine worship. Zechariah revealed four basic principles that illustrate how faith reveals itself in practical and ethical ways:

- Administer true justice.
- Show mercy.
- Do not oppress persons in need (widows, the fatherless, strangers, the poor).
- Do not think evil of, or plot against your neighbor.

See also Zechariah 8:16–17 for a similar statement. Sometimes good teachers repeat themselves. Such was the case for this prophet. Furthermore, a cursory reading of other prophets in the Old Testament reveals similar commands toward others.

Neighbors Make a Difference (Matthew 5:13–16)

Early in his ministry with the disciples, Jesus looked at them and said, "You are the salt of the earth" (Matt. 5:13) and "You are the light of the world" (Matt. 5:14). I can imagine Simon Peter thinking, *Me? That's incredible.* Jesus had a high estimate and ambition for his disciples.

Salt works quietly, it is essentially invisible. Light is open and visible. Salt preserves and enhances. Light reveals, points the way, and may warn of impending trouble. Jesus said his disciples were to be both. What confidence he had in them. He has the same confidence in us. We, too, are salt and light.

We face the constant challenge of getting our "salt" out of the shaker and getting our "light" into the world. That's why we as believers must be intentional in our lifestyle. Salt does not just lose its saltiness; it becomes less salty when it is diluted with impurities or contaminating agents. Salt was not created to stay in the shaker. Similarly, Christians are not saved to merely remain in the church house. Light helps us see where we are and guides us to where we should go. Light does not get extinguished, but it can be covered. If this occurs it loses its power to impact the darkness or lead one to where the light of the world (Jesus) wants us to be.

If salt and light are fulfilling their purposes, people will notice. Jesus indicated that when others notice our good deeds they need to see beyond us to God himself. We have an awesome privilege and responsibility—to be a window through which people can see God. Though some might want to give us praise, we should always strive to give God any credit or honor.

Don't forget the arena for salt and light—the earth and the world. We are not a "secret service" organization; rather we are devoted to making a difference in our sphere of influence, sometimes quietly and sometimes visibly. We meet to worship, but we leave the worship center to enter the arena of service, making a difference in our neighborhood and beyond.

Implications and Actions

Our communities are blessed with people we know as "first responders." These public servants—fire fighters, police officers, EMTs, and other medical personnel—protect us and help us. In much the same way, we as believers can be first responders in our neighborhoods. We can be the first people to provide a good word about God. We can be the first to invite someone to church, to welcome new persons, to express sympathy, to encourage, and to care. Our world is becoming less community-oriented, whether we live in a suburban gated neighborhood or a rural county seat town. However, if we take Scripture seriously, we can be a neighbor who is not only a first responder, but one who also stays faithful to the end in serving those in our community.

Consider the outline headings used in this Bible study. Look for ways to implement these: neighbors practice the basic ten; neighbors love neighbors; neighbors do the right thing; and neighbors make a difference. When you are a good neighbor, you encourage others to do the same, and a genuine community grows.

QUESTIONS

1. When it comes to putting your faith into practice, what motivates you more—emotions or commandments? Are you prone to do something when you feel like it, or because God commands it? Explain.

2. How do you help a person who says he hates someone in his heart (Lev. 19:17)?

3. "Blessed are the weak" is not one of the beatitudes in the New Testament, but your neighborhood may contain weak, needy, hurting, or overlooked people who may believe they are oppressed and overwhelmed by life. How can you care for these neighbors who are struggling to live a better life? How can your class reach out to the underserved populations in your area?

4. How can Jesus' teaching about salt and light help a person overcome low self-esteem?

5. Salt can become diluted because of impurities. What impurities might dilute your witness to your neighbors? What sins or attitudes might be covering up your light in your community?

FOCAL TEXT
Ephesians 6:5–9;
Colossians 3:22–25;
1 Timothy 6:1–2; Titus 2:9–11

BACKGROUND
Ephesians 6:5–9;
Colossians 3:22–25;
1 Timothy 6:1–2; Titus 2:9–11

MAIN IDEA
Our work ethic reflects
our devotion to Christ.

QUESTION TO EXPLORE
What does my work
ethic reveal about my
devotion to Christ?

STUDY AIM
To evaluate what my work
ethic reveals about my
devotion to Christ

QUICK READ
Most of our adult life is spent
in the workplace. Whether we
are an employer or employee,
our lifestyle at work should
reflect our commitment
to Christ and his values.

LESSON NINE
Employer

Introduction

A pastor told me, "I enjoy everything about the pastorate except the people." A friend said, "I like the people where I work, but I can't stand my job." Sometimes we have a hard time finding a life that balances people and work, responsibility and reward. Making a living is sometimes not easy; however, if we seek to bring honor to Christ through our vocation, we have a better possibility of enjoying the people around us as well as our work.

EPHESIANS 6:5–9

[5] Slaves, obey your earthly masters with respect and fear, and with sincerity of heart, just as you would obey Christ. [6] Obey them not only to win their favor when their eye is on you, but like slaves of Christ, doing the will of God from your heart. [7] Serve wholeheartedly, as if you were serving the Lord, not men, [8] because you know that the Lord will reward everyone for whatever good he does, whether he is slave or free.

[9] And masters, treat your slaves in the same way. Do not threaten them, since you know that he who is both their Master and yours is in heaven, and there is no favoritism with him.

COLOSSIANS 3:22–25

[22] Slaves, obey your earthly masters in everything; and do it, not only when their eye is on you and to win their favor, but with sincerity of heart and reverence for the Lord. [23] Whatever you do, work at it with all your heart, as working for the Lord, not for men, [24] since you know that you will receive an inheritance from the Lord as a reward. It is the Lord Christ you are serving. [25] Anyone who does wrong will be repaid for his wrong, and there is no favoritism.

1 TIMOTHY 6:1–2

[1] All who are under the yoke of slavery should consider their masters worthy of full respect, so that God's name and our

teaching may not be slandered. [2] Those who have believing masters are not to show less respect for them because they are brothers. Instead, they are to serve them even better, because those who benefit from their service are believers, and dear to them. These are the things you are to teach and urge on them.

TITUS 2:9–11

[9] Teach slaves to be subject to their masters in everything, to try to please them, not to talk back to them, [10] and not to steal from them, but to show that they can be fully trusted, so that in every way they will make the teaching about God our Savior attractive.

[11] For the grace of God that brings salvation has appeared to all men.

Background: Slavery

Paul frequently used the word "slaves" to describe Christians. The Greek word is sometimes translated as "servants," perhaps to make it easier for modern Christians to understand and accept. Many of us may not know much about either slaves or "servants," but we do have a distaste for anything that appears to condone slavery.

In the New Testament world, slavery was a fact of life. Slavery in that time was not based on race, but rather upon the economy. Some estimate that sixty million slaves lived within the Roman Empire during this time. Who knows the correct number, but the truth is that persons living then did not have the employment options that are available in the 21st century. Some people lived their entire lives as slaves in order to meet the basic needs of their families—food, clothing, and housing.

Many Christians were probably slaves; some were masters. Though the New Testament did not condemn slavery, the gospel contained the seeds that eventually would confront racial slavery and help persons to see the sinfulness of treating people as possessions. Slavery was outlawed 150 years ago in America, but we still feel the impact of that sordid period of our history when we practiced and condoned racial slavery.

As a biblical word, however, "slave" can be helpful to us. Jesus called us "friends" (John 15:15). However, we are also slaves of Jesus; utterly committed to him to do all that he wants us to do. He is our Master, the Lord of our lives. The slave mindset stands in stark contrast to the casual Christianity often practiced today.

Slave and Master, Employee and Employer (Ephesians 6:5–9)

Though you might not identify readily with being a "slave" or following a human master, you understand the relationship between employee and employer, manager, boss, or supervisor. These verses provide sound principles on which to develop a work ethic that can be mutually beneficial, not only between employees and employers, but also to society as a whole. You can also apply these principles to the way you serve God in and through your church.

The first principle comes from the phrase "Slaves, obey your earthly masters" (6:5). Today, this could be summarized as: do what you were hired to do. That is the basic understanding of obeying your employer. Obviously, if your supervisor is trying to lead you into sin, that is another issue, but such a situation is usually the exception, not the typical work experience. Paul linked obedience with respect, fear, and sincerity. Remember that your employer can hire someone else if you do not do the job you were hired to do.

The second principle is to work as if you are trying to please God (6:6). When an employee works well, the employer or boss is pleased. For the Christian, pleasing others is important but secondary. The primary motivation for all things is to please God and to do his will. Some people work diligently when the supervisor is around but slack off when no one is watching. Such laziness should not characterize Christians. We want to please the boss, but ultimately we want to please God and honor him with our work ethic.

The third principle is to work wholeheartedly (6:7). Work is labor, but it should be done with a positive attitude and with full energy. We should give our best efforts, not just punching a clock or going through the motions. No one can give a one hundred and ten percent, but we should work hard and well. The first-century slave may not have had a choice but to work well. Regardless of the circumstance (the slave's life was not easy), Paul expected slaves to give their best effort.

The fourth principle is that good work will be rewarded (6:8). A person may be a slave or free, an employee or employer, but good work does not go unnoticed, least of all by God. Your paycheck is your earthly reward for good work. Some people may chafe at their work circumstances and income levels, but that can be evaluated and negotiated. However, this verse reminds believers that if you seek God's approval of your work, then you will have the blessing and reward of God. In other Scripture (Galatians 6:7), Paul taught about "sowing and reaping," and that is an additional reward that comes when you do your job well. Hard work reaps rewards, both monetary and otherwise.

Though verses 5–8 pointedly address slaves and employees, verse 9 solely speaks to masters or employers. Just as God rewards those who serve well, earthly masters and employers should do the same. The workplace should be worker-friendly, not a place for intimidation, threats, and immoral behavior. At this point in Scripture, Paul alluded to a simple and profound teaching that was a significant change to the accepted views of Christian people in the first century. He wrote that God does not discriminate. God is the ultimate Master, and as such, he views earthly slaves and masters as equal.

God does not play favorites because of social, economic, family, or racial status—and neither should we. Earlier in Galatians 3:28, Paul wrote, "There is neither Jew nor Greek, slave nor free, male or female, for you all are one in Christ Jesus." Also read Acts 10 for the remarkable story of Peter and Cornelius in the early days after Jesus' ascension to heaven. Peter confessed, "I now realize how true it is that God does not show favoritism but accepts men from every nation who fear him and do what is right" (Acts 10:34–35). Whether you are an employee, boss, manager, or owner, we all serve an impartial God who loves us regardless of our job title or position. God set the pattern for how we are to love and treat each other.

Slaves and Masters (Colossians 3:22–25)

The Colossian passage essentially reiterates the Ephesians passage. Christians often need to be reminded about essential principles, so Paul

THE NEW TESTAMENT AND SLAVERY

In the first century, slavery was practiced in most countries and among many occupations, including teachers, manual laborers, soldiers, doctors, and house servants. Some people criticize Christianity because neither Jesus nor the early church condemned slavery. However, at that time, slavery bore little resemblance to the racial slavery that has plagued Western Civilization and America for many years.

The guiding principle in Ephesians is "submit to one another out of reverence for Christ" (6:21). Then Paul applied mutual submission to home life as well as to slaves and masters (5:22—6:9). Paul challenged Christians and culture, but he was not attempting to incite a social uprising in the first century that would burn hot for a while but soon fade away. Paul's goal was to build the church of Jesus Christ, one that would then change lives and history. Thus, when the church remained faithful to its calling and teaching, the power of the gospel helped change society and bring an end to slavery.

included this principle in both letters. In Ephesians and Colossians these instructions are set in the context of what is sometimes referred to as a "household code." Some aspects of the household code are similar to the accepted views of Roman society at the time, but Paul challenged those standards. In Ephesians, Paul challenged both husbands and masters to follow the central principle of being mutually submissive to their wives and slaves, respectively (Eph. 5:21). In Ephesians and Colossians, Paul gave slaves rights and masters responsibilities that came from God—their ultimate Master in heaven.

Notice four phrases in Colossians that echo Paul's teaching in the passage from Ephesians. These phrases highlight the spiritual nature of the slave-master relationship, as well as the Christian's work in the world and the local church:

- Reverence for the Lord
- Working for the Lord
- Inheritance from the Lord
- The Lord you are serving

This subject actually concludes in Colossians 4:1, with a strong admonition for masters (employers and managers). In this verse, Paul wrote, "Masters, provide your slaves with what is right and fair, because you know that you also have a Master in heaven." In the first century, masters were often not held accountable to anyone, and slaves had few rights. Paul countered that thinking by proposing that all people are accountable to God (Romans 14:12). Masters will be held responsible for doing what is right and fair. They also need to follow the four principles outlined in these verses: revere the Lord; work for the Lord; know that God will reward you; and serve the Lord. These principles are true for both slaves (employees) and masters (employers).

Showing Respect (1 Timothy 6:1–2)

Sometimes athletes and celebrities complain that they "get no respect." Usually that outcry is accompanied by some accomplishment that they think deserves recognition, or they may complain that someone is getting more attention or pay than they are. Regardless, their plea is for attention and recognition—respect. That sense of entitlement and self-centeredness receives little or no encouragement in Scripture.

When it comes to respecting others, however, slaves (employees) should respect the role of the master (employer). Labor and management may be convenient categories, but they do not have to be adversarial. In his day, Paul was aware of persons who were "eye pleasers" and perhaps went through the motions of working while not reflecting the presence and Spirit of Christ.

Paul gave Timothy two reasons for respecting masters: the negative impact on God's name and Christian teaching when slaves disrespect their master (6:1); and the fact that some masters and slaves are fellow believers (6:2). Evidently, some Christian slaves were presuming on their relationship with Christian masters, and not serving them with the quality of work that was best for the master or household.

Putting a Good Face on Faith (Titus 2:9–11)

Paul and Peter were pillars of the early church. Both impacted their

PHILEMON AND ONESIMUS

The short New Testament book of Philemon provides a case study in how Paul's teaching applies in a real-life situation. Paul loved both Philemon (a master) and Onesimus (a slave). He called Philemon his dear friend and fellow worker (Philemon 1:1), as well as brother. He called Onesimus his son (1:10), saying Onesimus was his very heart (1:12). Onesimus had run away from Philemon and had become a Christian while on the lam. He helped Paul, who was imprisoned in Rome (1:11), but Paul sent Onesimus back to Philemon (1:12). Under Roman law, Philemon could have severely punished or killed Onesimus. Paul asked Philemon to accept Onesimus back without retribution and to receive him as a brother instead (1:15–16).

world through their witness and writing. They wrote about similar topics and highlighted similar themes. One example is Peter's writing about how one person can influence another by the quality of life that a Christian demonstrates (1 Peter 2:12, 15; 3:1, 16). Sometimes, influencing others happens without saying a word. Paul may have used different language, but he also stressed the importance of living rightly so that one's conduct brings honor to Christ and the church. Both slaves and masters are under the same obligation, though the book of Titus focuses more on the largest group among church members—the slaves.

Paul instructed Titus to teach slaves to embrace subjection and not to rebel against it. Thus, Titus challenged believers to try to please their masters, and not talk back, steal, or do anything that would create mistrust. The passage closes with the result (as well as the motivation) of this good behavior: to "make the teaching about God our Savior attractive" (2:10b). Before others can see Christ, they may first need to see him in his followers.

Implications and Actions

Christians work in all kinds of situations. Likewise, we work with all kinds of people, some of whom profess faith in Christ and some who do not. Both have a work ethic, but some may have no knowledge of how Christians should behave as an employee or a boss. In the diversity of the workplace, Christians have a special opportunity to reveal our relationship to Christ by the quality of our character and work.

As you consider the various Scriptures that form this study, consider how well you reveal Christ in the work you perform. Modeling Christ transcends the workplace, because Christians do not have one persona for work, one for play, and one for worship. We should have a consistent character that can be revealed in any setting, whether we are an employee or employer. Your life should be a window through which people see Christ.

QUESTIONS

1. If your fellow employees made a list of people who do the best job at revealing Christ through their work, would your name be on the list? Why or why not?

2. How can you influence others to please God by the way they live and work?

3. How can you use the earthly rewards of your work (your salary) to declare the gospel?

4. What are you doing in your church that reflects a work ethic that is pleasing to God?

5. Who in your workplace needs your expression of respect?

LESSON TEN
Government

FOCAL TEXT
Romans 13:1–7;
1 Timothy 2:1–4

BACKGROUND
Romans 13:1–7;
1 Timothy 2:1–4

MAIN IDEA
We are to pray for and
submit to our governmental
authorities.

QUESTION TO EXPLORE
Do I pray for and submit to
my governmental authorities?

STUDY AIM
To commit to pray
for and submit to my
governmental authorities

QUICK READ
As Christians, we should relate
to governmental authority
in ways that please God and
allow us to be good citizens.

Introduction

Love undergirds every issue that affects Christians; thus, we begin our discussion of how we relate to governmental authority with the question of love. What does love have to do with how I relate to my government? What does love have to do with taxes, voting, laws, and political figures? When you turn to Romans 13:1–7, look at the verses preceding and following this selection of Scripture. You will find that this teaching about governmental authority is "bookended" by Romans 12, which uses thirteen verses to explain the nature of love that is sincere and genuine (Rom. 12:9–21). On the other side, Romans 13:8 speaks of our "continuing debt to love one another." Love means bringing out the best in one another, and good citizenship can do that. Trust God for placing this passage of Romans where it is. Our responsibilities as citizens need to be understood in the context of love and how genuine love behaves within the context of obeying the government.

ROMANS 13:1–7

[1] Let every person be subject to the governing authorities; for there is no authority except from God, and those authorities that exist have been instituted by God. [2] Therefore whoever resists authority resists what God has appointed, and those who resist will incur judgment. [3] For rulers are not a terror to good conduct, but to bad. Do you wish to have no fear of the authority? Then do what is good, and you will receive its approval; [4] for it is God's servant for your good. But if you do what is wrong, you should be afraid, for the authority does not bear the sword in vain! It is the servant of God to execute wrath on the wrongdoer. [5] Therefore one must be subject, not only because of wrath but also because of conscience.

[6] For the same reason you also pay taxes, for the authorities are God's servants, busy with this very thing. [7] Pay to all what is due them—taxes to whom taxes are due, revenue to whom revenue is due, respect to whom respect is due, honor to whom honor is due.

1 TIMOTHY 2:1–4

¹ First of all, then, I urge that supplications, prayers, intercessions, and thanksgivings be made for everyone, ² for kings and all who are in high positions, so that we may lead a quiet and peaceable life in all godliness and dignity. ³ This is right and is acceptable in the sight of God our Savior, ⁴ who desires everyone to be saved and to come to the knowledge of the truth.

People Under Authority (Romans 13:1–5)

God ordained authority—even governmental authority. The ultimate authority to which we submit is God, but God has ordained government as one of the higher authorities to which we align our lives. Most of us understand the adjustments we make to obey authority. As a child, we adjusted our behavior to comply with our parents' rule and authority, or else we faced the consequences. Submitting to authority continued as we obeyed leadership in school and the community. We obey leadership in the workplace. Ideally, we come to realize that we are responsible to various authorities and accountable for our actions. Government is one of those authorities that God established to help us live in an orderly civilization. Unfortunately, our prisons are filled with people who have not practiced good citizenship and have not learned to submit to authority for the well-being of society.

Having a governing authority does not mean that every type of government or governmental figure is God's perfect will for us. I am confident that God took no delight in Nazism or many other totalitarian governments through the ages or those present today. Not every government is good, and some people use governmental authority abusively. In New Testament times, misused governmental authority led Peter and John to say that believers must obey God rather than people (Acts 4:19). They rebelled against the civil authority when that authority contradicted God's word. Gratefully, we in the U.S. have been spared much of that kind of governmental intrusion, but many in our world do not experience freedom from abusive government, while others suffer the effects of poor citizenship.

In these verses, Paul challenged believers (then and now) to recognize the right of government to exercise authority in their lives. Paul affirmed God as the ultimate authority, and God has delegated authority to government. He elevated this principle when he wrote in verses 4 and 6 that this governing authority is God's servant. We are to be under that authority, seeking with government the common good of every person, and our country. As such, we embrace the principle of governmental rule, while also retaining the right to consider seriously the actions of the government.

Paul wrote to Christians in Rome, the seat of one of the most dominant powers in history. Later, Christians would be persecuted in the name of Roman law, and perhaps Paul himself was killed during the persecution of the Emperor Nero. Despite this persecution, Paul called for the people to live uprightly. He wrote, "rulers hold no terror to those

FIRST-CENTURY PERSECUTION

Life was not easy for the emerging first-century church. Jesus' popularity and message threatened the status quo of the Jews, so many began to look for ways to kill him. They and the Romans eventually executed Jesus, but his death was not the final word. God raised him from the dead; however, persecution of Christians continued. Jewish religious leaders were the early instigators of persecution and caused the deaths of early church leaders, including Stephen and James. Once Christians began to grow in number, the Roman government was the chief persecutor. Paul and Peter died for their faith. Various emperors led the persecution, with Nero (A.D. 54–68) and Domitian (A.D. 81–96) being especially brutal.

Against that background, much of the New Testament is written. Christians had no political leverage. However, they consistently taught on the major themes of today's Scripture. Believers honor Christ when they: 1) respect governmental authority; 2) do not behave in ways that bring negative attention to the faith; 3) pray for those in authority; 4) and share the gospel with all persons. Faithful living and evangelistic witness eventually helped change the atmosphere and the Roman Empire. Though our governmental system is vastly different, faithful witness and faithful living are still vital for the health of our country.

who do right, but for those who do wrong" (13:3). Paul did not want poor morality to reflect badly on God or fellow believers. The government can exercise its authority: if you do wrong, you will face punishment from the government, whether local, state, or federal (13:4).

We, as a nation, sometimes question whether the fear of punishment is a deterrent to crime. However, I must admit that when I am driving and see a police car, I look at my speedometer. For me, the possibility of punishment deters wrong behavior. In encouraging submission to governing authority in verse 5, Paul wrote that believers submit for two reasons: 1) possible punishment; and 2) conscience. An orderly society needs the authority and power to restrain its citizens, which must also include the power to punish people who violate the life of a healthy society. Paul also appealed to conscience—the ingrained "rightness" of doing something simply because it is the right thing to do. Sometimes, doing the right thing gets you into trouble, but that is the exception and not the rule.

Remember, this lesson focuses on submitting to governing authority. The government is not God, though it has been ordained by God and thus has the right and responsibility to administer justice. The state is not infallible, but it is still to be respected. Persons of authority may not be worthy of our support, but the office he or she holds still deserves respect. God has ordained it. Pray that our governmental structures can live up to God's design and be God's servant across our land.

Duties of Good Citizens (Romans 13:6–7)

What can you do to help "governing authority" become good government? Be a good citizen. The Bible indicates that Christians have a dual citizenship (Philippians 3:2) in the kingdom of God and in the country in which they live. Just as we have obligations to God that we should fulfill, we also have obligations as citizens.

Paul mentioned four citizenship duties: taxes, tribute, respect, and honor. People should pay their taxes and bills, as well as show respect and honor to those who represent governing authority. Jesus commented on the tax issue. When asked by Pharisees if they should pay taxes, he told his listeners to give to Caesar what is Caesar's (tax) and give to God what belongs to him (Mark 12:17). Paul himself benefited from Roman

PRINCIPLES OF GOVERNMENTAL AUTHORITY AND GOOD CITIZENSHIP

- Governing authority is ordained by God. —Romans 13:1
- Citizens should not subvert government. —Romans 13:2
- Government will judge those who do evil. —Romans 13:2
- Government is entitled to tax for the common good. —Romans 13:2
- Honor and respect is due those who serve in governmental roles. —Romans 13:2
- Christians should pray for those in authority positions. —1 Timothy 2:1–2
- Good citizens who please Christ support government. —1 Timothy 2:1–2
- Government is blessed by the evangelistic efforts of Christian citizens. —1 Timothy 2:1–2

taxes. Tax money built roads that he used to spread the gospel. Roman citizenship and tax money provided him peace and protection, and Paul sometimes needed both (see Acts 21:35). Today, we often complain about taxes without appreciating fully the benefits we enjoy because of those taxes.

We enjoy many more citizenship privileges than people in biblical times. Often people ignore the opportunity and privilege of voting, but that certainly qualifies as a major blessing and responsibility. We can also become involved in local activities, participating in shaping our government and community in one capacity or another. Though we may not be shapers of public policy, we can all help determine who will lead in the implementation of governing authority. Many more of us should choose that option. Good citizens do not shirk such responsibility.

Respect and honor were important in ancient times, and they are important today as well. Many of us are good at criticizing government, but those who work in all areas of government are just people like you and me. From the lowest pay grade on up, government employees are representatives of governing authority, and as such, they deserve respect and honor. We live in a highly charged political world, but that is no excuse for unchristian behavior and words, which often paint a negative picture of government officials, even of those who serve faithfully and honorably.

Prayer for Those in Authority (1 Timothy 2:1–4)

Jesus prayed for many people, sometimes with dramatic results. He also prayed for us (see John 17:20). Thus, it is not surprising that God would lead Paul to teach the followers of Jesus to pray for others. Sometimes our prayers are of a "God bless everybody" generality. Notice in these verses how Paul began praying—for rulers and governmental authority. He got specific. Those who serve God as they work in governmental roles should be the focus of our prayers on a continual basis—not just during election season.

When we discuss governing authority, it's easy to debate theoretical situations in which Christians cannot and should not submit to governmental authority. These situations sometimes occur and we should discuss them, but don't miss the main point in these two verses—pray for those who exercise governmental authority. Some of these people may not represent your political viewpoint; indeed some may even be considered political enemies. However, Jesus challenged his disciples to pray for their enemies (Matthew 5:44–45; Luke 6:27–28). Jesus taught that the peacemakers would be known as the children of God (Matthew 5:9). Certainly his teaching should affect any point of view, question, or situation we face.

Paul mentions a second responsibility in these verses—to live peaceful lives that reflect godliness and holiness. There is no set pattern for applying these verses in a diverse world filled with both goodness and evil. Paul himself struggled. He was run out of more towns than most people, but he continued to practice and preach a lifestyle that was both courageous and peaceful. In American society, we are blessed to live under the protection of the Bill of Rights, as well as the daily protection we enjoy through civil authority.

Paul wrote that praying for those in authority and living a peaceful lifestyle pleases God. Paul set this teaching in the context of God's eternal purpose. Our behavior should reflect a changed life brought about by

Christ. God uses holy and godly lives to draw others to himself, including government officials. Remarkably, how you respond to authority in all areas can be a deterrent to the Christian faith or it can draw people to it.

When we pray for everyone, especially those in governing authority, what should be the content of our prayers? Certainly, we pray that God would grant them wisdom and guidance. We pray for their ability to lead our country and government. We can pray that they would come to know the truth of the gospel. We can pray for all kinds of concerns. We want all the blessings of good government, so we ask God to work to create a strong and functioning civil structure. However, our prayer life is incomplete if we do not pray for the salvation of those in government authority. They need a genuine and personal relationship with God through Jesus Christ. They need our prayer for their growth in Christ. Have you prayed for the salvation of those who exercise governing authority in your community? In your state? In the nation?

Implications and Actions

Americans experience so many blessings because of our system of government. No system is flawless and neither is anyone in authority. However, our lives are far better because of the wisdom and courage of those who have gone before us in establishing our governmental structure.

Christians should be prime examples of good citizenship. People who love God and love one another should lead the way in following basic principles of government and praying for those who carry them out. Both ancient and modern law concentrate on what we should not do, but Christians must also be concerned about what we should and can do. We follow laws not just to stay out of jail, but also because we want all people to live well and enjoy life. We seek to do good for others, and as a result, we will reap blessings for ourselves. We can be good citizens of the kingdom of God and the country in which we live.

QUESTIONS

1. Which aspect of being a good citizen is most difficult for you to put into practice?

2. If Paul were writing today about your responsibility as a citizen, what would he say?

3. What responsibilities do Christians have when government becomes abusive or does not fulfill its purpose in seeking the good of all?

4. How are the principles of being a good citizen similar to those of being a good church member?

5. What do you need to do differently in light of today's Bible study?

FOCAL TEXT

Ephesians 4:11–16;
1 Thessalonians 5:12–13;
Hebrews 13:17–18

BACKGROUND

Ephesians 4:11–16;
1 Thessalonians 5:12–13;
Hebrews 13:17–18

MAIN IDEA

We are to respect, support, and submit to our spiritual leaders as they guide us to build the body of Christ.

QUESTION TO EXPLORE

Do I respect, support, and submit to my spiritual leaders in the church?

STUDY AIM

To evaluate my attitudes and actions toward the spiritual leaders in my church

QUICK READ

In a culture in which authority is questioned and leadership is scrutinized at every turn, this lesson reminds believers to love and support their church leaders.

LESSON ELEVEN
Church Leaders

Introduction

A story is told about a man who woke up one Sunday morning and told his wife, "Honey, I don't want to go to church today. The people there don't like me. They complain all the time, talk behind my back, and criticize me when I make a mistake." The wife patted her husband's hand, and said, "You *have* to go to church this morning. You're the pastor."

Unfortunately, some ministers—paid and volunteer—feel as if their church spends more time criticizing them than encouraging them. From the time they walk in the door on a Sunday morning (or Wednesday or . . .) they are bombarded by people who want something from them. Prayer requests. Complaints about the temperature in the sanctuary. Calls to visit someone who feels like the staff hasn't been paying enough attention to them. Sunday school leaders who failed to get a substitute while they were on vacation.

The relationship between church leaders and church members is to be characterized by Christlike love—with both parties accountable to God for their attitudes, words, and actions. While being a church leader can be a daunting, exhausting, and overwhelming role, this lesson reminds us to encourage, respect, and honor our leaders as appointed by God in their role to lead his church.

EPHESIANS 4:11–16

11 It was he who gave some to be apostles, some to be prophets, some to be evangelists, and some to be pastors and teachers, 12 to prepare God's people for works of service, so that the body of Christ may be built up 13 until we all reach unity in the faith and in the knowledge of the Son of God and become mature, attaining to the whole measure of the fullness of Christ.

14 Then we will no longer be infants, tossed back and forth by the waves, and blown here and there by every wind of teaching and by the cunning and craftiness of men in their deceitful scheming. 15 Instead, speaking the truth in love, we will in all things grow up into him who is the Head, that is, Christ. 16 From him the whole body, joined and held together by every supporting ligament, grows and builds itself up in love, as each part does its work.

1 THESSALONIANS 5:12-13

¹² Now we ask you, brothers, to respect those who work hard among you, who are over you in the Lord and who admonish you. ¹³ Hold them in the highest regard in love because of their work. Live in peace with each other.

HEBREWS 13:17-18

¹⁷ Obey your leaders and submit to their authority. They keep watch over you as men who must give an account. Obey them so that their work will be a joy, not a burden, for that would be of no advantage to you. ¹⁸ Pray for us. We are sure that we have a clear conscience and desire to live honorably in every way.

Learn from Your Leaders (Ephesians 4:11–16)

This section of Scripture is set within Paul's discussion of the unity and diversity within the body of Christ. These verses explain how God has structured the church for maximum growth and ministry. First, God has given some people specific gifts related to leadership within the church—apostles, prophets, evangelists, pastors, and teachers. Other places in Scripture (Romans 12:6–8; 1 Corinthians 12:8–10, 28–30) list additional spiritual gifts, but here Paul focused on those specifically related to church leadership. Some of these roles, like apostles and prophets, are typically not recognized in most churches today (see large sidebar), but the other gifts still play a significant part in the church. You won't see a growing church that lacks this kind of ongoing leadership.

Second, Paul explained the ongoing task of those church leaders (Eph. 4:12). Men and women in leadership are charged with the task of training believers in the church to do the work of the church. Unfortunately, many people form a distorted view of leadership within church. I've overheard some church members say, "I don't check on visitors. That's what we pay the pastor to do." This view—all too common in the local church—clearly distorts God's purpose for creating leadership roles in the church.

Leaders train the body of Christ so that everyone within the body is equipped to carry out all of the work of the church, whether it is evangelism, discipleship, or administration. God never intended for the paid (or volunteer) church staff to do all of the work of the church. That responsibility falls on *every* believer, not just a select few.

Third, Paul explained the result of such training and work. The body of Christ grows and matures toward unity. One common reason for arguments and disharmony in the church is because its members have not grown past infancy in their spiritual lives. While they may have been Christians for years, they may have yet to mature in their faith under the leadership of their local church.

Rather than grow in their faith and stretch their spiritual muscles, they "sit and soak" on Sunday morning and never move beyond that point. They think their sole responsibility is to occupy a pew, put a twenty-dollar bill in the offering plate, and occasionally attend Sunday school. Clearly, this passage challenges believers to move to deeper levels of spiritual maturity and to be engaged in the life and ministry of the church.

Fourth, Paul gave a description of what an immature believer (and church) looks like. Such believers are "infants" who are deceived easily and believe every religious teaching, even if it is not biblical. From

APOSTLES

The word "apostle" means "one who is sent." In the New Testament, the term was used in at least two distinct ways. The term initially referred to the twelve disciples sent out by Jesus to share the gospel message with the world. After his resurrection, the term became synonymous with someone who had seen Jesus' ministry from his baptism to his resurrection (Acts 1:21–22). Having seen Christ on the road to Damascus, Paul was one of the main apostles named in the New Testament. Others were named as apostles, but only in the sense that they had been sent out by God (Acts 14:4; Romans 16:7; 1 Thessalonians 2:6). Most churches today do not use the term "apostle" to identify leaders within its congregation.

ideas about angels to the theology of heaven and hell, many immature believers will believe anything because they have not been sufficiently discipled, and their faith has no anchor.

In contrast to this, Paul described in verses 15–16 what believers become as they mature. They "grow up" in Christ. Together, with others within the body of faith, each believer does his own work in service to Christ. This results in a mature believer and a mature church.

Honor Your Leaders (1 Thessalonians 5:12–13)

In addition to writing to the church at Ephesus, the Apostle Paul also wrote a letter to the church in Thessalonica. Although written to different audiences, both letters address church leadership. In these verses, Paul challenged the believers to "respect those who work hard among you" (v. 12). Notice that Paul didn't ask believers to always agree with leaders. You will disagree with them. Nevertheless, you can demonstrate respect.

Respecting your leaders means that you don't talk bad about them as you drive home from church. Respect means listening to their sermons instead of critiquing their speaking styles. Respect means recognizing their God-given authority to lead the church instead of trying to undermine them behind the scenes.

Paul also told his readers to "hold them in highest regard." Simply speaking, this means that you should value those in leadership and not take them for granted. Unfortunately, sometimes church members take advantage of church leaders rather than esteem them or value them. Perhaps this is because church leaders often work behind the scenes, doing work that many will never know about. And perhaps, church members don't value their leaders because those leaders do their work without the need for applause or recognition.

Many church leaders are incredibly humble. They are called by God and know they are following his will, and that is enough for them. However, this passage is clear: recognize your leaders for their service. Honor them for their unending ministry. Value their gifts and skills and concern for the church body. Everyone needs encouragement, love, support, and respect—even church leaders.

Follow and Pray for Your Leaders (Hebrews 13:17–18)

At the end of this book, the writer of Hebrews (nobody knows for sure who that was) provided a few last-minute, practical instructions for believers. In these verses, the writer reminded believers about how to treat spiritual leaders. The instructions are simple: obey them; submit to them; pray for them.

In today's individualistic culture, obeying church leadership can frustrate the average American. Our culture tells us to buck the system, challenge authority, make your own path, go against the flow, refuse to be confined by conventional boundaries. Yet, the writer's instruction is clear—obey your leaders. You probably won't agree with every decision they make. You may not understand why they respond to certain situations in a particular manner.

Your individual personalities may clash. In fact, you might not even want to be friends with some of the leaders in the church because you are so different and disagree on so many issues. However, keep in mind that God has ordained those leaders to be in those roles for this time, and God calls you to obey them. Follow the instructions offered in their sermons and lessons. Follow their examples and imitate their faith (Hebrews 13:7) as they imitate Christ (1 Corinthians 11:1).

Obviously, the writer was not advocating blind submission to leadership that is contrary to Scriptural truth. Even in the Old Testament, God pronounced judgment on religious leaders who failed to live and lead as God intended (Jeremiah 23:1; Ezekiel 34:1–4; Malachi 2:1–9). Jesus himself denounced the religious leaders because of their hypocrisy (Matthew 23:1–36; Luke 18:10–14). Church leaders have been called to a solemn task and are charged to carry out their roles with exemplary character and integrity. In these verses, however, the writer focused on the responsibility of believers to submit to their leaders, assuming that those leaders were submitted to and seeking after Christ.

Why should you submit to your church leaders? Because they have been charged with the task of keeping watch over you. They care about what happens to the people under their care, including you! They understand that they will be held accountable to God for their leadership and direction, so they take their roles seriously. Rather than making their lives miserable by arguing every petty point or disagreeing with them

PROPHETS

In the Old Testament, prophets spoke for God to the people of Israel and to individuals as well. They called for Israel to honor and follow God. Often, they would predict (foretell) an event in the future, such as the Babylonian threat spoken of in Jeremiah and Ezekiel. In the early church, however, the role of a prophet changed. Instead of being foretellers of the future, prophets were "forth-tellers" of truth. They spoke truth with clarity as directed by God. This role in the church can be seen today in people who speak the truth of God into a specific situation within the church body.

over issues that don't really matter eternally, believers are called to obedience so that their ministry will be a joy and not a burden. Just as leaders are held accountable for their leadership, individual believers are responsible for their "follow-ship."

The most important gift you can give your church leadership is prayer on their behalf. Because of their role, church leaders face opposition from the devil, who longs to thwart the work of God at every turn. The next time you are tempted to criticize the leadership in your church for not doing something right, for not recognizing you, or for forgetting small details, turn those negative critiques into prayers. Ask God to help them "live honorably" (Heb. 13:18) and to conduct their lives in a godly, Christ-honoring manner. Ask God to protect them and their families against the attacks of the enemy. Ask God to give them favor in the community with civic leaders and other religious leaders. Ask God to show you how you can support your leaders. You'd be surprised at how quickly your attitude may change.

Implications and Actions

This week, take notice of how you treat the staff members and other leaders in your church. Are you quick to judge them? Or are you quick to pray for them? Ask yourself why you may be at odds with those who lead your congregation. You may discover a radical truth: the problem isn't something that the leaders have done, but rather your own attitude

toward these leaders. Ask God to reveal to you the changes you may
need to make in order to treat leaders as he has commanded.

QUESTIONS

1. Put yourself in the place of the leaders in your church. What do
   you think their lives and ministry are like?

2. What do you think is the overall attitude toward the leaders in
   your church?

3. Over what issues do you see the church membership and
   leadership possibly clashing?

4. How can your Bible study class show support for your church
   leadership?

5. Who among your church leadership is often forgotten or
   overlooked? How could you support and encourage them?

FOCAL TEXT

Acts 4:32–37;
1 Corinthians 12:12–27;
Galatians 6:9–10;
Hebrews 10:24–25

BACKGROUND

Acts 4:32–37;
1 Corinthians 12:12–27;
Galatians 6:9–10;
Hebrews 10:24–25

MAIN IDEA

Christ followers gather
regularly to encourage,
serve, and sacrifice for the
church and each other.

QUESTION TO EXPLORE

What are my responsibilities
to my fellow Christians?

STUDY AIM

To commit to gather regularly
to encourage, serve, and
sacrifice for my church and
my fellow Christians

QUICK READ

Being involved in a faith
community has become an
option in today's culture rather
than a commitment. Christ
followers must remember their
calling to engage with fellow
Christians on a regular basis.

LESSON TWELVE
Fellow Christians

Introduction

"I love Jesus, but I can't stand the church."
"You don't have to be a part of the church to be a Christian."
"The church is full of hypocrites."
Have you ever heard these statements? Have you ever spoken them? Unfortunately, many believers have experienced the *worst* the church has to offer rather than its best. As a result, they have given up on the church and refuse to invest themselves in this vital, yet imperfect aspect of the Christian life. Christ loved the church (Ephesians 5:25), even though its members are sinful and fallible. This lesson outlines the role of the church in the life of a Christ follower as it explores our relationships with other Christians.

ACTS 4:32–37

[32] All the believers were one in heart and mind. No one claimed that any of his possessions was his own, but they shared everything they had. [33] With great power the apostles continued to testify to the resurrection of the Lord Jesus, and much grace was upon them all. [34] There were no needy persons among them. For from time to time those who owned lands or houses sold them, brought the money from the sales [35] and put it at the apostles' feet, and it was distributed to anyone as he had need.

[36] Joseph, a Levite from Cyprus, whom the apostles called Barnabas (which means Son of Encouragement), [37] sold a field he owned and brought the money and put it at the apostles' feet.

1 CORINTHIANS 12:12–27

[12] The body is a unit, though it is made up of many parts; and though all its parts are many, they form one body. So it is with Christ. [13] For we were all baptized by one Spirit into one body— whether Jews or Greeks, slave or free—and we were all given the one Spirit to drink.

[14] Now the body is not made up of one part but of many. [15] If the foot should say, "Because I am not a hand, I do not belong

to the body," it would not for that reason cease to be part of the body. [16] And if the ear should say, "Because I am not an eye, I do not belong to the body," it would not for that reason cease to be part of the body. [17] If the whole body were an eye, where would the sense of hearing be? If the whole body were an ear, where would the sense of smell be? [18] But in fact God has arranged the parts in the body, every one of them, just as he wanted them to be. [19] If they were all one part, where would the body be? [20] As it is, there are many parts, but one body.

[21] The eye cannot say to the hand, "I don't need you!" And the head cannot say to the feet, "I don't need you!" [22] On the contrary, those parts of the body that seem to be weaker are indispensable, [23] and the parts that we think are less honorable we treat with special honor. And the parts that are unpresentable are treated with special modesty, [24] while our presentable parts need no special treatment. But God has combined the members of the body and has given greater honor to the parts that lacked it, [25] so that there should be no division in the body, but that its parts should have equal concern for each other. [26] If one part suffers, every part suffers with it; if one part is honored, every part rejoices with it.

[27] Now you are the body of Christ, and each one of you is a part of it.

GALATIANS 6:9–10

[9] Let us not become weary in doing good, for at the proper time we will reap a harvest if we do not give up. [10] Therefore, as we have opportunity, let us do good to all people, especially to those who belong to the family of believers.

HEBREWS 10:24–25

[24] And let us consider how we may spur one another on toward love and good deeds. [25] Let us not give up meeting together, as some are in the habit of doing, but let us encourage one another— and all the more as you see the Day approaching.

Believers Sacrifice for Each Other (Acts 4:32–37)

The Book of Acts reads like a biography. Rather than focusing on one person, however, Acts describes the birth and early growth of the church. It details the earliest days of the church and shows how Christianity spread to the known world because Christians courageously followed God's command to take the gospel to the ends of the earth (Matthew 28:19; Acts 1:8).

In these focal verses, Luke (who also wrote the Gospel that bears his name) described how the first Christians related to each other. He detailed a specific situation which demonstrates the love and harmony early believers demonstrated for each other. Verses 32–34 inform us that early Christians shared a common commitment to Christ and to each other that resulted in sharing their possessions with one another.

Verses 35–37 provide a concrete example of such selfless behavior through the life of a man named Joseph. He is best known by his nickname, "Barnabas," which means "son of encouragement." He sold a field and gave the money to the apostles, who were the leaders of the early church.

Scripture does not record why Barnabas gave the money, but it does tell us that his gift and the gifts of others were distributed to anyone who had need. Some early believers suffered hardship because of their faith in Christ. Some people refused to do business with Christians, who had abandoned the faith of their fathers (Judaism). Many Christians lost their jobs and their homes. Others were physically persecuted. One act of commitment and love practiced by these early Christians was sacrificially giving to help those who had been mistreated or victimized. The early church took care of one another.

In American culture, believers do not face persecution, but they do face hardship. Like the early church, Christians today have the opportunity to serve and give to fellow members who experience financial difficulty. For example, one of the members of my church was diagnosed with cancer last year. His time off for medical procedures, chemo and other treatments left his family in great financial need.

During this time, different members of our church have provided meals, donated airline tickets for travel to specialists, cared for their children, and given money so that this family could stay in their home. Such stories take place in countless churches both here and around the world. These beautiful acts of sacrifice show the world how the love of Christ can transform a group of people.

Believers Serve Each Other (1 Corinthians 12:12–27)

Chapter 12 of 1 Corinthians describes the role of spiritual gifts within the church. Paul compared the church to the human body. In verses 12–13, he reminded the believers that while people may differ in their cultural background or their spiritual gifts, Christ calls all believers together into one large group called the church. Different genders, one body of faith. Different spiritual gifts, one church. Different nationalities, one unified group built on Christ himself. Different places in society, one common God who brings them all together to occupy an equal place at the table of grace (Revelation 19:6–9).

In verses 14–20, Paul addressed a common problem in every group, not just churches. He wrote, "But in fact God has arranged the parts in the body, every one of them, just as he wanted them to be" (1 Cor. 12:18). Apparently, some believers dismissed their contribution to the church because their spiritual gifts weren't as visible or prominent as other gifts in the body. As a result, they concluded that their skills were not needed.

The same problem still takes place today. Some believers look at the gifts of the preacher or Sunday school teacher and think to themselves, "Wow. I could never do that. They are so gifted. I wish I had something like that to offer the church." Or a woman listening to reports about how church members shared Jesus on a mission trip may conclude, "I wish I could go on that trip next year, but I don't have the right skills or the gift of sharing Christ. I don't have anything to offer the group." In essence, Paul was calling everyone to service.

Think about Paul's argument. What would the church be like if only the pastor and teachers used their gifts to serve others? Who would offer mercy to those often left in the shadows? Who would serve behind the scenes and get the communion plates and cups ready? Who would keep the church running by using their gifts of administration?

Just like every part of the human body has a distinct function and role (12:15–19), without the contribution of every person within the church (from the pastor to the preschool worker), the church cannot fulfill its mission. You may think you don't have anything to offer your church, but you do. God promises that if you are a believer, he has given you gifts to use to serve others and to glorify him. You are not exempt from serving if your gifts happen to be less visible. You and your gifts have been placed in the body of faith for a purpose. When you use those gifts, you fulfill that purpose and honor the One who has bestowed your gifts.

Paul also addressed the other side of this coin: arrogance. In verse 21, he wrote, "The eye cannot say to the hand, 'I don't need you!' And the head cannot say to the feet, 'I don't need you!'" If you have ever been around children, you have heard this familiar declaration of independence. "I can do it myself." "I don't need your help." "Let me try!"

This striving for autonomy is a natural part of human development. However, as we get older, we must also learn another important truth: we can't do everything by ourselves. We need others. Arrogant and immature believers are quick to cover up their needs and try to find a solution on their own. However, the Scripture is clear—Christianity is

THE BOOK OF HEBREWS

Both the writer of Hebrews and the context in which it was written are a bit of a mystery. Both have been the subject of much debate since the second century. In some of the early manuscripts, Paul's name is mentioned in the title, but the writer never inserts his name anywhere within the letter. The writer also omits the recipients of the letter and where they lived. However, the text does reveal clues about its author. First, he (or she) had extensive knowledge of the Old Testament. The book contains dozens of references to that early canon.

Second, the writer was well-educated. The Greek used in the letter, along with the vocabulary and sentence structure, shows both a solid grasp of the language and a creative touch. Third, the writer cared about his readers. Throughout the book, the author repeatedly challenged his readers to remain faithful and steadfast in their commitment to Christ.

Several New Testament characters (besides Paul) have been suggested as the writer of Hebrews, including Luke, Barnabas, Philip, Jude, Apollos, and even Priscilla. In the end, only God knows the real writer, and regardless of whom that person was, God is the ultimate Author as he inspired the writer to pen the letter. The truths contained in the book do not lose their significance simply because the writer is unknown.

to be expressed in a shared community. You were never meant to go it alone. God created the body of Christ so that each person's unique gifts could contribute to the common good.

Believers Do Good Even When Weary (Galatians 6:9–10)

Not too long ago, I decided to get into shape by training for a 5K run. I purchased some good running shoes, clothes, and an app for my phone to track my progress. Early on in my training, I learned an important principle: sometimes you just have to grind it out. Most runners (even newbies like me) talk about "hitting the wall"—that moment in time when your legs stop working, your brain screams "Stop!" and you think you can't take another step. The only way past that wall is to push through it. You just keep running, one foot in front of the other, until you feel good again and finish the run.

In Galatians 6:9–10, Paul reminded the church (and us) to keep going, even when the going is tough. Giving to others, being a light in a dark world, caring for the forgotten, and giving a cup of cold water in Jesus' name can be exhausting. You will "hit the wall." That is, you will want to give up, walk off, walk out, quit going.

The remedy is to keep going—with a little help along the way. When we come together as a body of believers, we remember the end result of doing good, of not giving up on each other. We see it in the young adults who remained faithful through their teen years and now serve in student ministry. We reap the rewards when new people find a relationship with Jesus. We are renewed when someone walks up and says, "You're doing a great job. Thanks for what you do." Those moments provide fuel for our race, reminding us to keep going, to keep doing good, and to keep loving and serving each other.

Believers Meet Together Regularly and Encourage Each Other (Hebrews 10:24–25)

Paul: "Hey, Bob, how ya doing?"

Bob: "Doin' good, Paul. Doin' good. How are you?"

Paul: "Fine, thanks."

Bob: "Well, great! See ya later, Paul."

How many times have you participated in a conversation like this when you walked through the church on a Sunday morning? All of us are guilty of offering platitudes and pat answers when people ask us how we are. In the church, though, we should be able to be honest with each other. We should be able to share our burdens, hurts, failures, and discouragements, as well as our joys with our fellow Christians. We need to encourage each other to stay the course.

The writer of Hebrews (see sidebar) understood this, and spoke about it in Hebrews 10. In verses 24–25, believers are reminded to keep meeting together regularly, prodding each other along in loving and serving others, and encouraging each other to hold onto the hope found in Christ.

The writer understood that Christians cannot encourage each other if they don't see each other on a regular basis. That is why meeting together as a body of believers is so critical. It's not about high attendance Sunday

APPLYING THE LESSON THIS WEEK

1. Write a letter to someone who has used his or her gifts to serve you. Thank him (or her) for how their service has encouraged you.

2. When you are at church this week, ask someone, "How are you?" After the person's response, say, "No, really, how are you?" and listen intently to the reply. Make an effort to minister to that person.

3. Find a way to serve behind the scenes in your church. Pick up the trash in the sanctuary, help fold bulletins, or write a note to a shut-in.

4. If you have never taken a spiritual gifts test, find one online to take or ask your pastor for a resource he would recommend. Upon discovering (or rediscovering) your gift(s), seek opportunities to use it in ministry.

or a good report at the annual convention. Meeting together and encouraging each other are essential elements in staying true to our faith in the midst of a sinful world.

Implications and Actions

Sitting around a campfire, you can see a principle of spiritual growth. The embers that remain closest to the fire remain strong, bright, and warm. They produce the most heat. Those embers that get separated or pushed away from the fire become cold quickly and will eventually fade out into ash.

In much the same way, spending time with fellow Christians is like being an ember close to the fire. You absorb the heat from those around you and continue to burn strongly and brightly as you influence other believers and the lost world for Christ. Staying away from the church—and individual believers—will leave you cold, without vibrancy and without light. You will eventually fade out and lose your passion. You need other Christians. And other Christians need you.

QUESTIONS

1. How have you seen Christians sacrifice for each other?

2. How have fellow believers used their gifts to serve you recently? How have you served others?

3. Why do you think it is difficult to accept others' service to us? Why do we try to fix our problems ourselves rather than rely on the gifts of others to help us?

4. How have you reaped a reward for continuing to do good and serving those in the church?

5. How would you respond to a person who made statements like the ones in the Introduction?

FOCAL TEXT

2 Corinthians 5:11–21;
1 Peter 3:15–16;
Colossians 4:2–6

BACKGROUND

2 Corinthians 5:11–21;
1 Peter 3:15–16;
Colossians 4:2–6

MAIN IDEA

Christians are called to be
ministers of reconciliation.

QUESTION TO EXPLORE

Do I seek to be a minister
of reconciliation in
my relationships with
non-Christians?

STUDY AIM

To seek to be a minister
of reconciliation in
my relationships with
non-Christians

QUICK READ

One of the most challenging
aspects of living in a secular
world is relating to non-
Christians. Christ followers
are to serve as ambassadors
who speak on behalf of Jesus.

LESSON THIRTEEN
Non-Christians

Introduction

At a restaurant one day, I was talking with the server about the best days of the week to work. I guessed correctly that the most coveted shift was Saturday night. The most hated shift? Sunday afternoon and evening. Why? Because, in her experience, "church people are rude and demanding and they give bad tips."

Unfortunately, her experience isn't an isolated occurrence. Many non-Christians don't want to go to church because of the way church people treat them. This lesson is a reminder about how believers ought to relate to those who don't know Christ.

2 CORINTHIANS 5:11–21

[11] Since, then, we know what it is to fear the Lord, we try to persuade men. What we are is plain to God, and I hope it is also plain to your conscience. [12] We are not trying to commend ourselves to you again, but are giving you an opportunity to take pride in us, so that you can answer those who take pride in what is seen rather than in what is in the heart. [13] If we are out of our mind, it is for the sake of God; if we are in our right mind, it is for you. [14] For Christ's love compels us, because we are convinced that one died for all, and therefore all died. [15] And he died for all, that those who live should no longer live for themselves but for him who died for them and was raised again.

[16] So from now on we regard no one from a worldly point of view. Though we once regarded Christ in this way, we do so no longer. [17] Therefore, if anyone is in Christ, he is a new creation; the old has gone, the new has come! [18] All this is from God, who reconciled us to himself through Christ and gave us the ministry of reconciliation: [19] that God was reconciling the world to himself in Christ, not counting men's sins against them. And he has committed to us the message of reconciliation. [20] We are therefore Christ's ambassadors, as though God were making his appeal through us. We implore you on Christ's behalf: Be reconciled to God. [21] God made him who had no sin to be sin for us, so that in him we might become the righteousness of God.

1 PETER 3:15–16

[15] But in your hearts set apart Christ as Lord. Always be prepared to give an answer to everyone who asks you to give the reason for the hope that you have. But do this with gentleness and respect, [16] keeping a clear conscience, so that those who speak maliciously against your good behavior in Christ may be ashamed of their slander.

COLOSSIANS 4:2–6

[2] Devote yourselves to prayer, being watchful and thankful. [3] And pray for us, too, that God may open a door for our message, so that we may proclaim the mystery of Christ, for which I am in chains. [4] Pray that I may proclaim it clearly, as I should. [5] Be wise in the way you act toward outsiders; make the most of every opportunity. [6] Let your conversation be always full of grace, seasoned with salt, so that you may know how to answer everyone.

Compelled by Christ's Love (2 Corinthians 5:11–15)

This passage takes place in the middle of one of Paul's letters to the church at Corinth. This church, like many today, struggled with divisions inside the church as well as conflict with the outside world. Unlike other churches, however, the church at Corinth often squabbled with Paul and questioned his authority as one sent by God. Several times in this letter he defends his role within the early church (2 Cor. 1:1; 2:17—3:2; 5:12–13).

In verse 11, Paul explained the reason behind his passion for sharing Christ with both Jews and Gentiles: the fear of the Lord. Paul was not afraid of God's judgment if he failed to spread the gospel, rather, he understood the wrath that no longer awaited him because of Christ's sacrifice, and he was awestruck by this. Apart from Jesus, Paul (and all of us!) was a target of God's terrible wrath. Knowing that others would experience such righteous wrath motivated Paul to persuade people to turn to Christ.

Paul's mission drove him with such passion and focus that he reminded the Corinthian church that he was of his right mind (v. 13). This was not the first time his mental status had been questioned. In Acts 26, during Paul's exchange with King Agrippa, Festus told Paul that he was out of his mind (26:24).

To the Jewish people, Paul must have seemed to be out of his mind. To believe that an itinerant preacher from Nazareth was actually the long-awaited Messiah must have seemed like the most unlikely change of heart, especially since Paul had been such a well-known and respected leader among the Jews. Not only that, but Paul had continued to believe and spread this new religion even though it meant personal suffering and sacrifice. Perhaps this is why Paul felt led to tell the Corinthians that his seemingly deranged behavior had a divine source—God himself, the One who had radically changed Paul's heart and life.

In the next breath, Paul gave a secondary reason for such unorthodox behavior—the church at Corinth. Simply put, Paul was out of his mind because of them, out of his care and love for them. Paul felt "compelled" by Christ's love. The message of the gospel compelled him. The love of God demonstrated on the cross drove him. He could not stop his ministry to the Corinthians.

In some ways, his words echo those of the ancient prophet Jeremiah who said, "But if I say, 'I will not mention him or speak any more in his name,' his word is in my heart like a fire, a fire shut up in my bones. I am weary of holding it in; indeed, I cannot" (Jeremiah 20:9). Such a fire burned in Paul, a fired fueled by Christ's love. Christ's love for people had become Paul's love for people. He was "convinced" that this One had died for all people—including the Corinthian believers, even though those believers could be cantankerous, disagreeable, self-seeking, and carnal.

Such love also compels believers today. The greatest motivator in sharing the gospel is a deep understanding of one's sinfulness before God, and a deep gratitude that God would forgive and save sinners, even though we deserve God's full and rightful wrath. As Jesus said of the woman who had anointed his feet with precious perfume, "her many sins have been forgiven—for she loved much. But he who has been forgiven little loves little" (Luke 7:47).

Christians have been forgiven much—much more than we can possibly comprehend on this side of heaven. Such love for God, coupled with a love for people who need to know about God's grace and mercy through Jesus Christ, should compel us to tell others about him. Unfortunately, many people feel guilty and are shamed into sharing, which leaves them even more ashamed when their efforts don't result in immediate conversions. Sharing how much Christ loves people and how he died for them (2 Cor. 5:14–15) will come across much more genuine when that love is the motivating factor for talking about Jesus.

Sent With a Message (2 Corinthians 5:16–21)

Paul not only talked about God's love as the motivating factor for sharing the gospel, but he also talked about the message itself. Verses 16–21 contain different aspects of the gospel: "if anyone is in Christ, he is a new creation" (v. 17); "God . . . reconciled us to himself through Christ" (v. 18); through Christ, God is not "counting men's sins against them" (v. 19); "Be reconciled to God" (v. 20). The end of the chapter culminates with a crescendo of mystery: "God made him who had no sin to be sin for us, so that in him we might become the righteousness of God" (v. 21). This passage contains the story of the gospel in a mere six verses.

1, 2, AND 3 CORINTHIANS?

The book of 1 Corinthians was not the first letter that Paul wrote to the Corinthian church. In 1 Corinthians, Paul stated, "I have written you in my letter" (5:9a), which indicates that Paul had written to this church before. The contents of the initial letter have been lost, but the text in 1 Corinthians gives clues about the first letter's contents.

The latter half of 1 Corinthians 5:9 tells the church "not to associate with sexually immoral people." This tells us that one issue in the actual first letter was the issue of living among sexually immoral people. Second, Paul's first letter to the Corinthian Christians was not taken seriously, because he addressed sexual immorality in 1 Corinthians (the second letter). In that second letter, he used the term, "now about" several times (7:25; 8:1; 12:1; 16:1, 12), indicating that he was responding to the church's response to the first letter. Apparently, the church had written with questions that Paul answered in 1 Corinthians, the second letter in this series of correspondence.

In verses 19–20, Paul explained the salvation message and our role in that message. God took the initiative to reconcile humanity to himself through the person and work of Christ. Because we are his people, Christ followers are charged with the task of being his ambassadors in our spheres of influence, both locally and globally.

In political terms, an ambassador acts as the representative of his home country in a special assignment, such as living in a foreign country speaking on behalf of the president. As Christians, we live not in a foreign country, but we are "aliens and strangers in this world" (1 Peter 2:11). We live on this earth as Christ's ambassadors, his representative on a special assignment—to speak a message on his behalf. The message is simple: "Be reconciled to God" (2 Cor. 5:20).

Be Prepared with Your Answer (1 Peter 3:15)

Peter wrote this book during a time of great religious and political upheaval. Politics and religion often intermingled, and at this point in history, Nero had ordered the persecution of Christians. Against this backdrop, Peter penned these words: "Though you have not seen him, you love him; and even though you do not see him now, you believe in him and are filled with an inexpressible and glorious joy" (1 Pet. 1:8). Such joy and hope must have seemed outrageous, even ludicrous, to outsiders who could not understand the reason for hope and joy in the

---

TO LIVE OUT THE LESSON THIS WEEK:

1. Ask God to open doors of opportunity for you to talk to others about your relationship with Christ.
2. Ask yourself: does God's love motivate me to share his love with others?
3. Choose to show love toward someone through a "random act of kindness."
4. In a journal, answer this question: Why do you believe in God?
5. Evaluate your life this week. What does your daily life say about what you believe?

midst of such suffering. In fact, the third chapter of 1 Peter, in which our focal passage sits, speaks about enduring suffering.

Peter challenged his audience to, "Always be prepared to give an answer" (1 Pet. 3:15) for the reason for such hope. This assumes that people would ask questions about such faith. Perhaps Peter had already experienced this cause-and-effect relationship between suffering and the demonstration of hope in its midst. Like other believers, Peter experienced his share of hardship in the name of Christ (tradition tells us he was crucified upside down), and such radical trust must have raised questions in the minds of people who had observed his life, particularly the change that Christ had brought.

The same challenge of readiness applies to believers today. While we may not suffer persecution in today's American culture, we will endure hardship. Such hardship will siphon and purify our faith, and that faith, coupled with hope despite the circumstances, will leave people wondering how we could possibly stand firm against the waves of adversity. We can give them a simple (yet profound) answer—we can endure the worst of life because we know that our hope lies in Christ and an eternity with him. Current suffering cannot compare with what awaits us beyond this life (Romans 8:18). We have hope because he is our hope.

Share with the Right Attitude and Lifestyle (1 Peter 3:15b–16)

After challenging believers to be prepared with an answer, Peter reminded them to share that answer with gentleness and respect for others. Apparently, such gentleness and respect were not always a part of the believers' speech. Unfortunately, Christians often have the same problem today. The headlines are scattered with stories of churches and individual Christians whose behavior demonstrates neither gentleness nor respect for others. While God can certainly use any situation to draw someone to himself, speaking to others with judgment and shame and condemnation does little to draw people to Christ. Perhaps this is why Peter emphasized the need for basic respect and a gentle approach when talking about one's faith.

To press home his point, Peter reminded his readers to have a clear conscience, meaning that their lives needed to reflect Christ and his love for others. This godly behavior would negate any lies or slander that a non-Christian might want to levy out of anger, bitterness, or spite. Peter's challenge reflects the quote often attributed to Ralph Waldo Emerson: "What you do speaks so loudly that I cannot hear what you say." If your actions do not reflect the beliefs you say you hold to, then your words are meaningless.

Pray and Look for an Opportunity (Colossians 4:2–6)

Like many of his other letters to churches, Paul's letter to the Colossian church focused on a variety of different topics, as Paul sought to help the church establish itself in a pagan culture. And like his other letters, this one contains prayer requests for both himself and for the church to whom he was writing.

In this passage, Paul asked the Colossian church to pray that God would open doors for the gospel message. He also asked the church to pray for him specifically, that he would tell the story of Christ with clarity. Two thousand years later, that same prayer applies to Christians. Sharing the mysterious message of a God who would redeem those who had rebelled against him requires God's working. Only God can open the door for you to talk about your faith. Only God provides the words. Only God provides the clarity. Only God is responsible for the outcome. Our responsibility, like Paul's, is to walk through the doors God puts before us. The rest is up to him.

In the midst of his prayer request, Paul turned his focus toward the church, giving them one last admonition: be wise. Use sound judgment and wisdom when talking to "outsiders," those who are not yet in the family of faith. His challenge echoes Peter's—"Let your conversation be always full of grace, seasoned with salt, so that you may know how to answer everyone" (v. 6). Again, the emphasis is on the way in which we share the gospel and not just the meat or message of the gospel. Responding to the love of God will be difficult if Christians tell the gospel story with judgment and condemnation. This passage brings us back to the very beginning of the lesson—God's love is what compels us to share. That same love should be evident in how we speak and how we live.

Implications and Actions

Which is more important: to share Christ verbally; or to live out an example that would draw people to ask about our faith? The answer is: both. As you experience God's transformative love, you cannot help but tell others about the depth and the lengths of God's grace, mercy, and forgiveness. However, as you share your experiences with others, they need to see a life that reflects your beliefs.

The combination of your verbal witness and your living example of faith is a powerful demonstration of how the love of God can change a life. When you share with others, treat non-Christians with the same tenacious love that drew you to Christ in the first place. Every person is looking for that kind of love, even if they don't recognize their need or desire for it.

QUESTIONS

1. If you were honest, what would you say motivates you to share the gospel with others? If not God's love, then what? (guilt, obligation, duty, etc.)

2. How have difficult experiences given you a platform for sharing your faith?

3. What would you say to someone who asked you why you follow Jesus?

4. What scares you most about sharing your faith with others?

5. What would *others* say is your attitude toward non-Christians? The server at lunch? The guy who changes your oil? Your family members? Your co-workers?

Our Next New Study
(Available for use beginning September 2015)

ROMANS: A Gospel-Centered Worldview

How to Order More Bible Study Materials

It's easy! Just fill in the following information. For additional Bible study materials available both in print and digital versions, see www.baptistwaypress.org, or get a complete order form of available print materials—including Spanish materials—by calling 1-866-249-1799 or e-mailing baptistway@texasbaptists.org.

Title of item	Price	Quantity	Cost
This Issue:			
Created for Relationships—Study Guide (BWP001197)	$3.95	_____	_____
Created for Relationships—Large Print Study Guide (BWP001198)	$4.25	_____	_____
Created for Relationships—Teaching Guide (BWP001199)	$4.95	_____	_____
Additional Issues Available:			
14 Habits of Highly Effective Disciples—Study Guide (BWP001177)	$3.95	_____	_____
14 Habits of Highly Effective Disciples—Large Print Study Guide (BWP001178)	$4.25	_____	_____
14 Habits of Highly Effective Disciples—Teaching Guide (BWP001179)	$4.95	_____	_____
Growing Together in Christ—Study Guide (BWP001036)	$3.25	_____	_____
Growing Together in Christ—Teaching Guide (BWP001038)	$3.75	_____	_____
Guidance for the Seasons of Life—Study Guide (BWP001157)	$3.95	_____	_____
Guidance for the Seasons of Life—Large Print Study Guide (BWP001158)	$4.25	_____	_____
Guidance for the Seasons of Life—Teaching Guide (BWP001159)	$4.95	_____	_____
Living Generously for Jesus' Sake—Study Guide (BWP001137)	$3.95	_____	_____
Living Generously for Jesus' Sake—Large Print Study Guide (BWP001138)	$4.25	_____	_____
Living Generously for Jesus' Sake—Teaching Guide (BWP001139)	$4.95	_____	_____
Living Faith in Daily Life—Study Guide (BWP001095)	$3.55	_____	_____
Living Faith in Daily Life—Large Print Study Guide (BWP001096)	$3.95	_____	_____
Living Faith in Daily Life—Teaching Guide (BWP001097)	$4.25	_____	_____
Participating in God's Mission—Study Guide (BWP001077)	$3.55	_____	_____
Participating in God's Mission—Large Print Study Guide (BWP001078)	$3.95	_____	_____
Participating in God's Mission—Teaching Guide (BWP001079)	$3.95	_____	_____
Profiles in Character—Study Guide (BWP001112)	$3.55	_____	_____
Profiles in Character—Large Print Study Guide (BWP001113)	$4.25	_____	_____
Profiles in Character—Teaching Guide (BWP001114)	$4.95	_____	_____
Genesis: People Relating to God—Study Guide (BWP001088)	$2.35	_____	_____
Genesis: People Relating to God—Large Print Study Guide (BWP001089)	$2.75	_____	_____
Genesis: People Relating to God—Teaching Guide (BWP001090)	$2.95	_____	_____
Exodus: Liberated for Life in Covenant with God—Study Guide (BWP001192)	$3.95	_____	_____
Exodus: Liberated for Life in Covenant with God—Large Print Study Guide (BWP001193)	$4.25	_____	_____
Exodus: Liberated for Life in Covenant with God—Teaching Guide (BWP001194)	$4.95	_____	_____
Ezra, Haggai, Zechariah, Nehemiah, Malachi—Study Guide (BWP001071)	$3.25	_____	_____
Ezra, Haggai, Zechariah, Nehemiah, Malachi—Large Print Study Guide (BWP001072)	$3.55	_____	_____
Ezra, Haggai, Zechariah, Nehemiah, Malachi—Teaching Guide (BWP001073)	$3.75	_____	_____
Psalms: Songs from the Heart of Faith—Study Guide (BWP001152)	$3.95	_____	_____
Psalms: Songs from the Heart of Faith—Large Print Study Guide (BWP001153)	$4.25	_____	_____
Psalms: Songs from the Heart of Faith—Teaching Guide (BWP001154)	$4.95	_____	_____
Jeremiah and Ezekiel: Prophets of Judgment and Hope—Study Guide (BWP001172)	$3.95	_____	_____
Jeremiah and Ezekiel: Prophets of Judgment and Hope—Large Print Study Guide (BWP001173)	$4.25	_____	_____
Jeremiah and Ezekiel: Prophets of Judgment and Hope—Teaching Guide (BWP001174)	$4.95	_____	_____
Amos. Hosea, Isaiah, Micah: Calling for Justice, Mercy, and Faithfulness—Study Guide (BWP001132)	$3.95	_____	_____
Amos. Hosea, Isaiah, Micah: Calling for Justice, Mercy, and Faithfulness—Large Print Study Guide (BWP001133)	$4.25	_____	_____
Amos. Hosea, Isaiah, Micah: Calling for Justice, Mercy, and Faithfulness—Teaching Guide (BWP001134)	$4.95	_____	_____
The Gospel of Matthew: A Primer for Discipleship—Study Guide (BWP001127)	$3.95	_____	_____
The Gospel of Matthew: A Primer for Discipleship—Large Print Study Guide (BWP001128)	$4.25	_____	_____
The Gospel of Matthew: A Primer for Discipleship—Teaching Guide (BWP001129)	$4.95	_____	_____
The Gospel of Mark: People Responding to Jesus—Study Guide (BWP001147)	$3.95	_____	_____
The Gospel of Mark: People Responding to Jesus—Large Print Study Guide (BWP001148)	$4.25	_____	_____
The Gospel of Mark: People Responding to Jesus—Teaching Guide (BWP001149)	$4.95	_____	_____
The Gospel of Luke: Jesus' Personal Touch—Study Guide (BWP001167)	$3.95	_____	_____
The Gospel of Luke: Jesus' Personal Touch—Large Print Study Guide (BWP001168)	$4.25	_____	_____
The Gospel of Luke: Jesus' Personal Touch—Teaching Guide (BWP001169)	$4.95	_____	_____
The Gospel of John: Believe in Jesus and Live!—Study Guide (BWP001187)	$3.95	_____	_____
The Gospel of John: Believe in Jesus and Live!—Large Print Study Guide (BWP001188)	$4.25	_____	_____
The Gospel of John: Believe in Jesus and Live!—Teaching Guide (BWP001189)	$4.95	_____	_____
The Gospel of John: Light Overcoming Darkness, Part One—Study Guide (BWP001104)	$3.55	_____	_____
The Gospel of John: Light Overcoming Darkness, Part One—Large Print Study Guide (BWP001105)	$3.95	_____	_____
The Gospel of John: Light Overcoming Darkness, Part One—Teaching Guide (BWP001106)	$4.50	_____	_____

Item	Price		
The Gospel of John: Light Overcoming Darkness, Part Two—Study Guide (BWP001109)	$3.55	_____	_____
The Gospel of John: Light Overcoming Darkness, Part Two—Large Print Study Guide (BWP001110)	$3.95	_____	_____
The Gospel of John: Light Overcoming Darkness, Part Two—Teaching Guide (BWP001111)	$4.50	_____	_____
The Book of Acts: Time to Act on Acts 1:8—Study Guide (BWP001142)	$3.95	_____	_____
The Book of Acts: Time to Act on Acts 1:8—Large Print Study Guide (BWP001143)	$4.25	_____	_____
The Book of Acts: Time to Act on Acts 1:8—Teaching Guide (BWP001144)	$4.95	_____	_____
The Corinthian Letters—Study Guide (BWP001121)	$3.55	_____	_____
The Corinthian Letters—Large Print Study Guide (BWP001122)	$4.25	_____	_____
The Corinthian Letters—Teaching Guide (BWP001123)	$4.95	_____	_____
Galatians and 1&2 Thessalonians—Study Guide (BWP001080)	$3.55	_____	_____
Galatians and 1&2 Thessalonians—Large Print Study Guide (BWP001081)	$3.95	_____	_____
Galatians and 1&2 Thessalonians—Teaching Guide (BWP001082)	$3.95	_____	_____
Letters to the Ephesians and Timothy—Study Guide (BWP001182)	$3.95	_____	_____
Letters to the Ephesians and Timothy—Large Print Study Guide (BWP001183)	$4.25	_____	_____
Letters to the Ephesians and Timothy—Teaching Guide (BWP001184)	$4.95	_____	_____
Hebrews and the Letters of Peter—Study Guide (BWP001162)	$3.95	_____	_____
Hebrews and the Letters of Peter—Large Print Study Guide (BWP001163)	$4.25	_____	_____
Hebrews and the Letters of Peter—Teaching Guide (BWP001164)	$4.95	_____	_____
Letters of James and John—Study Guide (BWP001101)	$3.55	_____	_____
Letters of James and John—Large Print Study Guide (BWP001102)	$3.95	_____	_____
Letters of James and John—Teaching Guide (BWP001103)	$4.25	_____	_____

Coming for use beginning September 2015

Item	Price		
Romans: A Gospel-Centered Worldview—Study Guide (BWP001202)	$4.25	_____	_____
Romans: A Gospel-Centered Worldview—Large Print Study Guide (BWP001203)	$4.50	_____	_____
Romans: A Gospel-Centered Worldview—Teaching Guide (BWP001204)	$4.95	_____	_____

Standard (UPS/Mail) Shipping Charges*			
Order Value	Shipping charge**	Order Value	Shipping charge**
$.01—$9.99	$6.50	$160.00—$199.99	$24.00
$10.00—$19.99	$8.50	$200.00—$249.99	$28.00
$20.00—$39.99	$9.50	$250.00—$299.99	$30.00
$40.00—$59.99	$10.50	$300.00—$349.99	$34.00
$60.00—$79.99	$11.50	$350.00—$399.99	$42.00
$80.00—$99.99	$12.50	$400.00—$499.99	$50.00
$100.00—$129.99	$15.00	$500.00—$599.99	$60.00
$130.00—$159.99	$20.00	$600.00—$799.99	$72.00**

Cost of items (Order value) _____

Shipping charges (see chart*) _____

TOTAL _____

*Please call 1-866-249-1799 if the exact amount is needed prior to ordering.

**For order values $800.00 and above, please call 1-866-249-1799 or check www.baptistwaypress.org

Please allow two weeks for standard delivery. For express shipping service: Call 1-866-249-1799 for information on additional charges.

YOUR NAME

PHONE

YOUR CHURCH

DATE ORDERED

SHIPPING ADDRESS

CITY

STATE   ZIP CODE

E-MAIL

MAIL this form with your check for the total amount to:
BAPTISTWAY PRESS, Baptist General Convention of Texas,
333 North Washington, Dallas, TX 75246-1798
(Make checks to "BaptistWay Press")

OR, **CALL** your order toll-free: 1-866-249-1799
(M-Fri 8:30 a.m.-5:00 p.m. central time).

OR, **E-MAIL** your order to: baptistway@texasbaptists.org.

OR, **ORDER ONLINE** at www.baptistwaypress.org.

We look forward to receiving your order! Thank you!